THE COOKERY COLLECTION

ORIGINAL AND DETAILED

500
RECIPES

Vegetarian

Everyday vegetarian recipes from quiches, soups
and pasta dishes to tarts, cakes and more

igloobooks

Published in 2018
by Igloo Books Ltd
Cottage Farm
Sywell
NN6 0BJ
www.igloobooks.com

LEO002 0218
2 4 6 8 10 9 7 5 3 1
ISBN 978-1-78810-195-0

All imagery: © iStock / Getty Images

Designed by Nicholas Gage
Edited by Richard Davis

Printed and manufactured in China

Contents

Brunches and lunches

Country vegetable soup

PREPARATION TIME: **5 minutes**
COOKING TIME: **20 minutes**
SERVES: **4**

2 tbsp olive oil
2 cloves of garlic, crushed
4 large tomatoes, chopped
2 large carrots, chopped
4 spring onions (scallions), chopped
2 courgettes (zucchinis), chopped
1 cauliflower, finely chopped
150 g / 5 oz / 1 cup peas, defrosted if frozen
1 litre / 1 pint 13 fl. oz / 4 cups vegetable stock
flat-leaf parsley, to serve

- Heat the oil in a saucepan and fry the garlic until softened.
- Add the tomatoes, carrots, spring onions, courgettes, cauliflower and peas to the pan and cook for 2 minutes, then stir in the vegetable stock and bring to the boil.
- Simmer for 10–15 minutes then season to taste with salt and pepper.
- Ladle the soup into 4 warm bowls and garnish with parsley.
- Delicious served with brown bread.

Smooth vegetable soup
Once cooked, blend the soup mixture with a liquidizer or hand blender for a smooth consistency.

Spicy guacamole

PREPARATION TIME: 10 minutes
SERVES: 4

2 large Hass avocados
1 lime
1 tbsp extra-virgin olive oil
½ red chilli (chili), seeds removed and chopped
fresh coriander (cilantro) leaves
tortilla chips, to serve

- Remove the stones from each avocado and scoop out the flesh.
- Mash the avocado flesh with the back of a fork until creamy but lumpy.
- Add the juice of half a lime, olive oil, chilli, coriander, a pinch of salt and black pepper.
- Stir well to combine and season to taste.
- Garnish with the remaining lime (cut into wedges), and some fresh coriander leaves.
- Serve with the tortilla chips.

Smoked paprika guacamole
Sprinkle some smoked paprika on the guacamole, alongside some dried chilli flakes for an extra spicy kick.

Beetroot borscht

PREPARATION TIME: 5 minutes
COOKING TIME: 40 minutes
SERVES: 4

2 tbsp olive oil
2 cloves of garlic, crushed
4 bulbs beetroot, finely chopped
1 litre / 1 pint 15 fl. oz / 4 cups vegetable stock
4 tbsp double (heavy) cream
a handful of baby chard, to garnish

- Heat the oil in a saucepan and add the crushed garlic. Once softened, add the chopped beetroot to the pan and cook for 2 minutes, then stir in the vegetable stock and bring to the boil.
- Simmer for 30 minutes then blend in a food processor or liquidizer until smooth.
- Taste the soup for seasoning and add salt and pepper as necessary.
- Ladle the soup into warm bowls and drizzle a spoonful of double cream on top of each one. Add a handful of baby chard leaves to garnish.

Butternut soup
Try roasted butternut squash instead of beetroot for a sweet and satisfying soup.

Fresh herb summer salad

PREPARATION TIME: 10 minutes
SERVES: 2

1 packet mixed leaf salad, washed
1 punnet red cherry tomatoes, sliced
1 punnet yellow baby plum tomatoes, sliced
1 bunch of fresh baby radishes, sliced
½ cucumber, sliced
1 small red pepper, sliced
fresh basil leaves, to garnish
fresh parsley leaves, to garnish
fresh coriander (cilantro) leaves, to garnish
½ lemon, sliced
2 tbsp lemon-infused extra-virgin olive oil

- Combine the salad leaves and all the ingredients in a large salad bowl.
- Toss the salad well to mix all the ingredients together.
- Drizzle over some oil and season to taste.
- Serve as a light lunch or a side salad.

Chickpea, pomegranate and couscous salad

PREPARATION TIME: **5 minutes**
COOKING TIME: **5 minutes**
SERVES: **2**

300 g / 10 ½ oz / 1 ¾ cups couscous
400 g / 14 oz / 2 ⅔ cups chickpeas (garbanzo beans), cooked
2 spring onions (scallions), chopped
1 pomegranate, seeds
fresh mint leaves, chopped

FOR THE DRESSING:
1 tsp runny honey
1 large orange, juiced
3 tbsp olive oil

• Put the couscous in a serving bowl and pour over 300 ml / 10 fl. oz / 1 ¼ cups of boiling water.
• Cover the bowl with cling film and let it stand for 5 minutes, then fluff up the grains with a fork.
• Stir the chickpeas, spring onions, pomegranate seeds and mint into the couscous.
• Whisk the honey, orange juice and olive oil together. Pour this dressing over the salad and serve.

Skinny sweet potato fries

PREPARATION TIME: **5 minutes**
COOKING TIME: **35–40 minutes**
SERVES: **4**

4 tbsp olive oil
800 g / 1 lb 12 oz sweet potatoes, cut into thin fries
½ lemon, juiced
1 pinch rock salt, to sprinkle
fresh flat-leaf parsley, to garnish
mayonnaise, to serve

• Preheat the oven to 220°C (200°C fan) / 425F / gas 7.
• Put the oil in a roasting tin and heat in the oven for 5 minutes.
• Tip the fries into the pan and turn to coat in the oil, then sprinkle with the lemon juice and rock salt.
• Bake the fries for 35–40 minutes, turning them every 15 minutes, until cooked through.
• Garnish with some parsley and serve with some mayonnaise.

Skinny potato fries
Replace the sweet potatoes with the same amount of normal cooking potatoes for classic fries. These are a great snack or side dish.

Black olive baguettes

PREPARATION TIME: **3 hours, 30 minutes**
COOKING TIME: **20–30 minutes**
MAKES: **2**

350 g / 12 oz / 2 ⅓ cups strong white bread flour,
plus extra for dusting

50 g / 1 ¾ oz / ⅓ cup stone-ground wholemeal flour

½ tsp easy-blend dried yeast

1 tbsp caster (superfine) sugar

1 tsp fine sea salt

1 tbsp olive oil

280 ml / 9 ¾ fl. oz / 1 cup warm water

75 g / 2 ⅔ oz / ½ cup black olives, pitted and roughly chopped

- Mix the flours, yeast, sugar and salt. Stir the oil into the warm water then stir it into the dry ingredients including the olives.
- Knead on a lightly oiled surface for 10 minutes.
- Leave the dough to rest, covered with oiled cling film, for 1–2 hours or until doubled in size.
- Roll the dough into 2 long baguettes and squeeze the ends into a point.
- Transfer the baguettes to a greased baking tray then cover with oiled cling film and leave to prove for 1 hour.
- Preheat the oven to 220°C (200°C fan) / 425F / gas 7.
- Dust the baguettes with a little flour and make diagonal slashes along the top with a sharp knife.
- Transfer the tray to the top shelf of the oven then bake for 20–30 minutes.

Sun-dried tomato baguettes
Replace the olives with the same quantity of chopped sun-dried tomatoes. Use the dried dehydrated variety (not in oil), and rehydrate by soaking in a bowl of hot water for 20 minutes.

Cauliflower soup

PREPARATION TIME: 5 minutes
COOKING TIME: 30 minutes
SERVES: 4

2 tbsp olive oil
2 tbsp butter
3 leeks, finely chopped
2 cloves of garlic, crushed
1 cauliflower, cubed
1 litre / 1 pint 15 fl. oz / 4 cups vegetable stock
100 ml / 3 ½ fl. oz / ½ cup double (heavy) cream
½ tsp freshly ground nutmeg
flat-leaf parsley, to garnish
a handful of chive stalks, to garnish

- Heat the oil and butter in a saucepan and fry the leeks for 8 minutes or until softened.
- Add the garlic and cauliflower to the pan and cook for 2 more minutes, then stir in the vegetable stock and bring to the boil.
- Simmer for 15 minutes then stir in the double cream and nutmeg.
- Blend the soup until smooth with a liquidizer or hand blender then try the soup and adjust the seasoning with salt and pepper.
- Garnish with some parsley and chives, then serve.

Coconut and cauliflower soup
Replace the butter with coconut oil and replace the cream with dairy-free coconut yogurt for a creamy vegan version.

Spiced carrot soup

PREPARATION TIME: **5 minutes**
COOKING TIME: **30 minutes**
SERVES: **4**

2 tbsp olive oil
1 onion, finely chopped
4 large carrots, julienne
1 tsp ground turmeric
1 tsp ground ginger
1 litre / 1 pint 15 fl. oz / 4 cups vegetable stock
a handful of fresh parsley leaves, chopped
coconut yogurt, to serve

- Heat the oil in a saucepan and fry the onion for 8 minutes.
- Add the carrots, turmeric and ginger to the pan and cook for 2 more minutes, then stir in the vegetable stock and bring to the boil.
- Simmer for 20 minutes then blend until smooth with a liquidizer or hand blender.
- Taste the soup and adjust the seasoning, then stir in half of the parsley and divide between 4 bowls.
- Top with the rest of the parsley and stir in some coconut yogurt to serve.

Spiced butternut soup
For an autumnal variation, replace the carrots with butternut squash. Remove the skin of 1 butternut squash and cut into cubes. Follow the same method or roast the squash in the oven for 20 minutes before blending.

Tomato, cucumber and lemon oil salad

PREPARATION TIME: **10 minutes**
SERVES: **2**

2 beefsteak tomatoes, chopped
½ red onion, diced
½ cucumber, diced
1 spring onion (scallion), chopped
2 tbsp extra-virgin olive oil
1 tsp balsamic vinegar
½ lemon, juiced
½ tsp pink peppercorns, crushed
1 pinch salt
1 tsp mixed herbs

- Combine the tomatoes, onion, cucumber and spring onions in 2 serving bowls.
- To make the dressing, mix the olive oil, balsamic vinegar, lemon juice, peppercorns, salt and mixed herbs.
- Pour over the salad and mix well, then serve.

Couscous and feta salad
Add some pre-cooked couscous and diced feta cheese to the salad for an equally appetizing light meal.

Pea and mint soup

PREPARATION TIME: 5 minutes
COOKING TIME: 15 minutes
SERVES: 4

2 tbsp olive oil
2 tbsp butter
1 onion, finely chopped
2 garlic cloves, crushed
400 g / 14 oz / 2 ⅔ cups peas, defrosted if frozen
1 litre / 1 pint 15 fl. oz / 4 cups vegetable stock
100 ml / 3 ½ fl. oz / ½ cup double (heavy) cream
1 tbsp mint leaves, finely chopped

- Heat the oil and butter in a saucepan and fry the onion for 5 minutes or until softened.
- Add the garlic and peas to the pan and cook for 2 more minutes, then stir in the vegetable stock and bring to the boil.
- Simmer for 5 minutes then stir in the double cream and mint.
- Blend the soup until smooth with a liquidizer or hand blender then try the soup and adjust the seasoning with salt and pepper.
- Ladle into warm bowls and stir in some double cream. Garnish with some fresh mint leaves.

Vegan pea and mint soup
For a vegan version of this delicious classic, follow the same method but omit the butter and replace the double cream with dairy-free coconut cream or yogurt.

Cheese and courgette scones

PREPARATION TIME: 10 minutes
COOKING TIME: 12–15 minutes
MAKES: 12

75 g / 2 ⅔ oz / ⅓ cup butter, cubed
250 g / 9 oz / 1 ⅔ cups self-raising flour, plus extra for dusting
½ tsp mustard powder
½ tsp cayenne pepper
150 ml / 5 ⅓ fl. oz / ⅔ cup milk, plus extra for brushing
2 medium-sized courgettes (zucchinis), grated
100 g / 3 ½ oz / 1 cup Cheddar cheese, grated
fresh basil leaves, to garnish

- Preheat the oven to 220°C (200°C fan) / 425F / gas 7 and line a baking tray with greaseproof paper.
- Rub the butter into the flour with your fingertips until the mixture resembles fine breadcrumbs then stir in the mustard powder and cayenne pepper.
- Add the milk, grated courgette and half of the cheese and mix together into a dough.
- Turn the dough out onto a floured work surface and flatten it into a rectangle, 2 cm (¾ in) thick.
- Use a round pastry cutter to stamp out the scones then transfer them to the baking tray.
- Brush the scones with milk, sprinkle with the rest of the cheese and bake for 12–15 minutes or until golden brown and cooked through.
- Transfer the scones to a wire rack to cool.
- Garnish with some fresh basil and serve.

Cheese and sun-dried tomato scones
Replace the grated courgette with 75 g / 2 ⅔ oz / ⅓ cup chopped sun-dried tomatoes. Add the tomatoes to the wet ingredients before forming the dough.

Home-made falafels

PREPARATION TIME: **10 minutes**
COOKING TIME: **8 minutes**
SERVES: **6**

2 tbsp sunflower oil
1 small white onion, finely chopped
1 clove garlic, crushed
400 g / 14 oz can chickpeas (garbanzo beans), washed and drained
1 tsp ground cumin
1 tsp ground coriander
a handful of fresh flat-leaf parsley, chopped
1 egg, beaten

- Heat a tablespoon of oil in a large pan then add the onions and garlic and lightly fry until the onion is soft and transparent.
- Tip into a large mixing bowl with the chickpeas and spices then mash together using a potato masher or the back of a fork.
- Stir in the parsley and season to taste. Add the egg then use your hands to bring the mixture together.
- Shape the mixture into small balls and flatten slightly using the back of a spoon. Heat the remaining oil in a pan then fry the falafels on a medium heat for 2–3 minutes on each side, or until golden brown.
- Once cooked, garnish with some fresh parsley and serve with some pitta and a dip of your choice.

Healthy cooked breakfast

PREPARATION TIME: **10 minutes**
COOKING TIME: **15 minutes**
SERVES: **4**

1 tbsp olive oil
1 bunch of fresh asparagus, lightly boiled
200 g / 7 oz / 1 ⅓ cups button mushrooms, sliced
8 eggs
fresh basil leaves, to serve

- Heat the oil in a non-stick frying pan until
  sizzling.
- Add the asparagus and the mushrooms to the
  pan and pan-fry until lightly browned.
- Crack the eggs into the pan and fry over a
  low heat until the eggs are slightly golden
  underneath.
- Once cooked, serve with some fresh basil
  leaves and season to taste.

Healthy breakfast with sourdough toast
Serve the eggs, asparagus and mushrooms with
a side of toasted sourdough bread for a filling
morning meal.

Cream cheese and dill crispbreads

PREPARATION TIME: 5 minutes
SERVES: 4

8 rye crispbreads
125 g / 4 ⅓ oz / ½ cup cream cheese
fresh dill, to garnish

- Top the crispbreads with the cream cheese.
- Garnish with short lengths of the fresh dill.
- Serve immediately.

Greek yogurt and dill crispbreads
For a lighter version, replace the cream cheese
with the same amount of Greek yogurt.

Baked potato with cottage cheese

PREPARATION TIME: **5 minutes**
COOKING TIME: **1 hour**
SERVES: **4**

4 medium baking potatoes
1 tbsp olive oil
4 tbsp cottage cheese
2 tbsp chives, chopped
1 pinch salt
1 pinch black pepper
4 radishes, stalks removed and sliced

- Preheat the oven to 200°C (180°C fan) / 400F / gas 6.
- Rub the potatoes with olive oil then place them on the top shelf of the oven.
- Bake the potatoes for 1 hour or until cooked through.
- Meanwhile, mix the cottage cheese, chives, salt and pepper.
- When the potatoes are ready, cut open the tops and spoon in the cottage cheese. Garnish each one with sliced radish and more chives.

Baked potato with guacamole
Replace the cream cheese with guacamole and a sprinkling of smoked paprika for a healthy and tasty alternative.

Deep-fried Camembert with cranberry sauce

PREPARATION TIME: **10 minutes**
COOKING TIME: **4–5 minutes**
SERVES: **6**

4 tbsp plain (all-purpose) flour
1 egg, beaten
75 g / 2 ⅔ oz / ½ cup breadcrumbs
2 Camembert, cut into small circles
sunflower oil, for deep-frying
cranberry sauce, to serve
salad leaves, to serve

- Put the flour, egg and breadcrumbs in 3 separate bowls.
- Dip the Camembert circles alternately in the flour, egg and breadcrumbs. Shake off any excess.
- Heat the oil in a deep-fat fryer, according to the manufacturer's instructions, to a temperature of 180°C / 350F.
- Lower the Camembert in the fryer basket and cook for 4 minutes or until crisp.
- Tip the Camembert into a kitchen-paper-lined bowl to remove any excess oil and serve with cranberry sauce and salad leaves.

Deep-fried Camembert with chutney
Replace the cranberry sauce with some delicious chutney for a tasty accompaniment.

THE COOKERY COLLECTION

Classic Greek salad

PREPARATION TIME: **10 minutes**
SERVES: **2**

1 iceberg lettuce, shredded
100 g / 3 ½ oz / ⅔ cup feta, cubed
6 medium tomatoes, quartered
½ cucumber, diced
½ red onion, finely sliced
a few Kalamata olives
4 tbsp extra-virgin olive oil
½ tsp pink peppercorns, crushed
1 tsp mixed herbs

- Arrange the shredded lettuce on 2 plates and top with the feta, tomatoes, cucumber, onion and olives.
- Drizzle with olive oil and sprinkle with the crushed peppercorns and mixed herbs.
- Serve immediately.

Greek salad with croutons
For added crunch, cut 2 slices of bread into squares. Add 1 tablespoon of olive oil to a pan and half a clove of crushed garlic, then lightly fry the croutons to the desired colour. Once cooked, leave to cool and season to taste.

Smoked hummus

PREPARATION TIME: **10 minutes**
SERVES: **4**

200 g / 7 oz / 1 ⅓ cups canned chickpeas (garbanzo beans), drained and washed
2 tbsp extra-virgin olive oil
1 clove garlic, crushed
½ lemon, juiced
1 tsp smoked paprika
fresh flat-leaf parsley, to garnish

- Add the chickpeas (reserve a few to garnish), olive oil, garlic, lemon and paprika to a blender and blitz, according to the manufacturer's instructions, until smooth. Add a little water if necessary.
- Spoon the hummus into a serving bowl and top with a little olive oil, some chickpeas and some smoked paprika.
- Season to taste and sprinkle some parsley on top before serving.

Pepper and lentil fajitas

PREPARATION TIME: **10 minutes**
COOKING TIME: **10 minutes**
SERVES: **4**

2 tbsp sunflower oil
1 onion, sliced
2 tbsp fajita seasoning
1 red pepper, sliced
1 yellow pepper, sliced
1 green pepper, sliced
a handful of cherry tomatoes, halved
400 g / 14 oz / 2 ⅓ cups cooked brown lentils
8 soft flour tortillas
fresh coriander (cilantro) leaves, to serve

- Heat the oil in a frying pan and stir-fry the onions with the fajita seasoning for 4–5 minutes.
- Add the peppers and tomatoes. Stir-fry for a further 4 minutes then add the lentils and mix well.
- Divide the mixture between the tortillas and add some fresh coriander leaves.

Pepper and quinoa fajitas
Replace the lentils with cooked quinoa for a healthy protein-packed meal.

Avocado, alfalfa and chilli toast

PREPARATION TIME: 5 minutes
COOKING TIME: 10 minutes
SERVES: 2

4 slices white sourdough bread
1 ripe Hass avocado, sliced
a handful of alfalfa sprouts
1 tsp chilli (chili) flakes
1 tsp sesame seeds
½ lemon, cut into wedges

- Preheat the grill to its highest setting.
- Toast the bread under the grill until golden brown.
- Cut the avocado in half and remove the stone and skin, then slice.
- Add the avocado slices, alfalfa sprouts and chilli flakes on top of the toast.
- Sprinkle with some sesame seeds and lemon juice and season to taste.
- Serve with a wedge of lemon.

Avocado and alfalfa on rye
Replace the sourdough bread with rye bread for a different taste and texture.

Cheese croquettes

PREPARATION TIME: **20 minutes**
COOKING TIME: **4–5 minutes**
MAKES: **16**

4 tbsp plain (all-purpose) flour
1 egg, beaten
75 g / 2 ⅔ oz / 1 cup breadcrumbs
450 g / 1 lb / 2 ½ cups mashed potato
250 g / 9 ½ oz / 1 cup green pesto
100 g / 3 ½ oz / 1 cup Cheddar cheese, grated
sunflower oil, for deep-frying
grated vegetarian Parmesan, to garnish
fresh basil, to garnish
1 lemon wedge, to garnish

- Put the flour, egg and breadcrumbs in 3 separate bowls.
- Mix the mashed potato with the pesto and Cheddar cheese then shape into 16 small balls.
- Dip the croquettes alternately in the flour, egg and breadcrumbs and shake off any excess.
- Heat the oil in a deep-fat fryer, according to the manufacturer's instructions, to a temperature of 180°C / 350°F.
- Lower the croquettes in the fryer basket and cook for 4–5 minutes or until crisp and golden brown.
- Tip the croquettes into a kitchen-paper-lined bowl to remove any excess oil.
- Serve hot with some vegetarian Parmesan, fresh basil leaves and a wedge of lemon.

Cheese and olive croquettes
Add some finely chopped black or green pitted olives to the potato and cheese mixture. Follow the method as above.

Potato and rosemary crisps

PREPARATION TIME: **35 minutes**
COOKING TIME: **6–7 minutes**
SERVES: **2–4**

600 g / 1 lb 5 oz Maris Piper potatoes
2–3 litres / 3 ½–5 pints sunflower oil
fresh rosemary, finely chopped
sea salt for sprinkling

- Cut the potatoes into very thin slices with a mandolin slicer or sharp knife.
- Put the slices in a bowl of cold water and leave them to soak for 25 minutes to remove some of the starch.
- Drain the potatoes and dry them completely with a clean tea towel.
- Heat the oil in a deep-fat fryer, according to the manufacturer's instructions, to a temperature of 130°C / 265F.
- Lower the potatoes in the fryer basket and cook for 5 minutes so they cook all the way through but don't brown. You may need to do this in batches so the fryer isn't overcrowded.
- Pull up the fryer basket and increase the temperature to 190°C / 375F.
- Cook the crisps at the hotter temperature for 1–2 minutes or until crisp and golden brown.
- Line a large bowl with a thick layer of kitchen paper and when the crisps are ready, tip them into the bowl to remove any excess oil.
- Leave to cool then sprinkle with sea salt and fresh rosemary.

Sweet potato crisps
Replace the Maris Piper potatoes with the same amount of sweet potatoes and follow the same method. Sprinkle with some salt and smoked paprika, then serve.

Smashed avocado on toast

PREPARATION TIME: 5 minutes
SERVES: 2

4 slices brown bread
1 ripe Hass avocado
½ lemon, juiced
a pinch of salt
6 cherry tomatoes, quartered
1 tsp chilli (chili) flakes
2 sprigs coriander (cilantro), chopped finely
½ lemon, wedges to garnish

- Preheat the grill to its highest setting.
- Toast the bread under the grill until golden brown.
- Cut the avocado in half and remove the stone and skin.
- Mash the avocado flesh with a fork and add some lemon juice and a pinch of salt.
- Spread generously on the toast and add some tomatoes, chilli flakes and chopped coriander leaves.
- Serve with a wedge of lemon for squeezing over the top.

Avocado and hummus on sourdough
Replace the brown bread with sourdough bread and add a dollop of plain hummus for a tasty alternative.

Four-seed wholemeal rolls

PREPARATION TIME: 3 hours, 30 minutes
COOKING TIME: 25 minutes
MAKES: 8

200 g / 7 oz / 1 ⅓ cups strong white bread flour, plus extra for dusting
200 g / 7 oz / 1 ⅓ cups malted granary flour
½ tsp easy-blend dried yeast
1 tbsp caster (superfine) sugar
1 tsp fine sea salt
3 tbsp poppy seeds
3 tbsp sesame seeds
3 tbsp flaxseeds
3 tbsp chia seeds
280 ml / 9 ¾ fl. oz / 1 cup warm water
1 tbsp extra-virgin olive oil

- Mix the flours, yeast, sugar, salt and seeds. Stir the oil into the warm water then stir it into the dry ingredients to make a dough.
- Knead the dough on a lightly oiled surface for 10 minutes.
- Leave the dough to rest, covered with oiled cling film, for 1–2 hours.
- Knead the dough for 2 more minutes, then shape into 8 large rolls.
- Transfer the rolls to a greased baking tray and cover again with oiled cling film. Leave to prove for 1 hour.
- Preheat the oven to 220°C (200°C fan) / 425F / gas 7.
- When the dough has risen, slash the tops with a sharp knife.
- Transfer the tray to the top shelf of the oven and bake for 25 minutes.

THE COOKERY COLLECTION

Asparagus and Parmesan frittata

PREPARATION TIME: 30 minutes
COOKING TIME: 35 minutes
SERVES: 6

8 eggs
1 tbsp crème fraiche
½ tsp dried basil
1 bunch of asparagus
1 onion, peeled and thickly sliced
2 tbsp olive oil
vegetarian Parmesan shavings, to serve
fresh basil leaves, to serve

- Preheat the oven to 180°C (160°C fan) / 350F / gas 4.
- Beat the eggs with the crème fraiche and dried basil in a large bowl.
- Snap the woody ends off the asparagus and discard. Cut the asparagus into short lengths.
- Fry the onion gently in olive oil for about 20 minutes, until golden and soft.
- Pour the egg mixture into the pan, add the asparagus and distribute evenly. Season with salt and pepper.
- Bake in the oven for about 35 minutes until puffed and golden. The egg should be cooked through.
- Cut into squares and serve with some Parmesan shavings and fresh basil on the side. Enjoy warm or cold.

Spinach and pea frittata
Replace the asparagus with a handful of chopped spinach and fresh or frozen peas. Serve with some fresh watercress on the side.

Tomato and cream cheese bagels

PREPARATION TIME: 5 minutes
COOKING TIME: 4 minutes
SERVES: 4

4 sesame wholemeal bagels
125 g / 4 ⅓ oz / ½ cup cream cheese
2 tbsp fresh dill, finely chopped
1 lemon, juiced
4 medium tomatoes, thinly sliced

- Heat a griddle pan until smoking hot. Slice the bagels in half and toast them on the griddle for 2 minutes on each side or until nicely marked.
- Mix the cream cheese with the dill and lemon juice and season to taste with salt and pepper.
- Spread the bottom half of the bagels with the cream cheese mixture and arrange the tomato slices on top.
- Position the other half of the bagels on top and serve while the bread is still a little warm from the griddle.

Red pepper and hummus bagels
Replace the cream cheese with the same quantity of plain hummus. Thinly slice 1 medium-sized red pepper and arrange on top of the hummus. Omit the dill and replace with chilli (chili) flakes.

Lemon and rosemary potatoes

PREPARATION TIME: **5 minutes**
COOKING TIME: **1 hour**
SERVES: **4**

800 g / 1 lb 12 oz potatoes, cut into chunks
3 sprigs of rosemary, roughly chopped
3 tbsp semolina (cream of wheat)
6 tbsp olive oil
2 lemons, juiced

- Preheat the oven to 200°C (180°C fan) / 400F / gas 6.
- Boil the potatoes in salted water for 10 minutes then drain well and leave to steam dry for 2 minutes.
- Toss the potatoes with the rosemary and coat with the semolina and season well with salt and pepper.
- Put the oil in a roasting tin in the oven to heat for 5 minutes. Add the potatoes to the roasting tin and spoon over the hot oil.
- Stir in the lemon juice, reserving 1 tablespoon. Roast the potatoes for 45 minutes or until golden brown, turning every 15 minutes.
- Once cooked, add the remaining tablespoon of lemon juice and mix well. Serve hot or cold.

Orange and rosemary potatoes
Replace the lemon juice with the same amount of orange juice. Juice one large orange, and reserve 1 tablespoon of the juice for serving.

Cream cheese and radish toast

PREPARATION TIME: 10 minutes
SERVES: 4

8 slices baguette
½ lemon, juiced
200 g / 7 oz / ¾ cup cream cheese
½ cucumber, sliced
4 radishes, sliced
½ tsp dried herbs
fresh parsley, to garnish

- Toast the baguette slices in a toaster or under a hot grill.
- Combine the lemon juice with the cream cheese and season to taste with salt and pepper.
- Spread the mixture onto the toast and add slices of the cucumber and radish.
- Top with some dried herbs and fresh parsley. Serve immediately.

White bean and garlic toast
Replace the cream cheese with a home-made white bean spread. Simply stir-fry 1 clove of crushed garlic in a pan with 2 tablespoons of olive oil. Add the white beans and mash to combine. Remove from heat, then add the juice of half a lemon and season to taste.

Egg and avocado muffin

PREPARATION TIME: **5 minutes**
COOKING TIME: **8–10 minutes**
SERVES: **2**

2 wholemeal muffins, halved
1 ripe Hass avocado
1 tbsp olive oil
2 eggs

- Preheat the grill to its highest setting.
- Toast the muffins under the grill until golden brown.
- Cut the avocado in half and remove the stone and skin.
- Slice the avocado and layer onto one of the muffin halves.
- Set the pan over a medium heat and add some oil. Crack the eggs one at a time and cook until the bottoms are fried and the yolk is still runny.
- Once cooked, transfer the fried eggs to the remaining half muffins and serve while still hot. Season with salt and freshly ground black pepper.

Egg and avocado sourdough
Replace the wholemeal muffins with sourdough bread and add a dollop of crème fraiche for a tasty alternative.

Red onion waffles

PREPARATION TIME: 10 minutes
COOKING TIME: 25 minutes
SERVES: 4

2 tbsp olive oil
1 red onion, finely chopped
250 g / 9 oz / 1 ⅔ cups plain (all-purpose) flour
2 tsp baking powder
2 large eggs
300 ml / 10 fl. oz / 1 ¼ cups milk
2 tbsp melted butter
sunflower oil, for oiling the waffle maker
vine cherry tomatoes, to serve
packet of rocket (arugula), to serve
crème fraiche, to serve
chives, to serve

- Put the oven on a low setting and turn on your electric waffle maker to heat up.
- Heat the oil in a frying pan and fry the onion for 5 minutes or until softened then season with salt and black pepper.
- Mix the flour and baking powder in a bowl and make a well in the middle.
- Break in the eggs and pour in the milk and fried onions then use a whisk to gradually incorporate all the flour from around the outside, followed by the melted butter.
- Spoon some of the batter into the waffle maker and close the lid. Cook for 4 minutes or according to the manufacturer's instructions, until golden and fully cooked through.
- Repeat until all the batter has been used, keeping the finished batches warm in the oven.
- Serve the waffles with the vine tomatoes, rocket, crème fraiche and chives.

Onion and herb waffles
Add 1 tablespoon of mixed dried herbs to the waffle mixture, ensuring the herbs are fully incorporated.

Beetroot hummus

PREPARATION TIME: **10 minutes**
SERVES: **4**

200 g / 7 oz / 1 ⅓ cups cooked chickpeas (garbanzo beans), drained and washed
200 g / 7 oz cooked beetroot, drained
2 tbsp extra-virgin olive oil
1 clove garlic, crushed
½ lemon, juiced
fresh flat-leaf parsley, roughly chopped

• Add the chickpeas (reserve a few to garnish), beetroot, olive oil, garlic and lemon to a blender and blitz until smooth and creamy. Add a little water if necessary.
• Spoon the hummus into a serving bowl and top with some chickpeas and some chopped parsley. Season to taste and serve with some toasted sourdough bread.

Spring vegetable medley

PREPARATION TIME: **5 minutes**
COOKING TIME: **25 minutes**
SERVES: **4**

2 tbsp olive oil
8 small salad onions, sliced
1 leek, finely sliced
400 g / 14 oz / 2 ⅔ cups garden peas, defrosted if frozen
175 ml / 6 fl. oz / ⅔ cup vegetable stock
1 tbsp crème fraiche

• Heat the oil in a large cast-iron casserole dish and lightly brown the onions and leeks. Add the peas to the pan and season with salt and pepper.
• Pour in the stock and bring to the boil and simmer for 5 minutes.
• Once cooked, stir in the crème fraiche and serve with some chunky bread or as a side dish.

Mini quiches

PREPARATION TIME: **40 minutes**
COOKING TIME: **40 minutes**
MAKES: **4**

2 tbsp olive oil
1 small onion, finely chopped
2 cloves of garlic, crushed
200 g / 7 oz tomatoes, chopped
200 ml / 6 ¾ fl. oz / ¾ cup vegetable stock
2 eggs, slightly beaten

FOR THE PASTRY
100 g / 3 ½ oz / ½ cup butter, cubed
200 g / 7 oz / 1 ⅓ cups plain (all-purpose) flour

FOR THE TOPPING
50 g / 1 ¾ oz / ½ cup Cheddar cheese, grated
parsley, to garnish

- Heat the oil and fry the onion and garlic for
  3 minutes. Add the tomatoes and stock and
  bring to a gentle simmer for 10–15 minutes.
- Meanwhile, make the pastry. Rub the butter
  into the flour and add just enough cold water
  to bind.
- Chill the pastry for 30 minutes then roll out
  on a floured surface.
- Preheat the oven to 200°C (180°C fan) / 400F
  / gas 6.
- Line the cases with pastry and prick with a
  fork. Then line the pastry with oven-safe cling
  film and fill with baking beans, then bake for
  10 minutes.
- In a medium bowl, combine the eggs and the
  cooled tomato mixture.
- Pour the mixture into the pastry cases
  once blind baked, then top with the grated
  Cheddar cheese.
- Bake the quiches for 20–30 minutes, or until
  a knife inserted into the middle comes out
  clean. Garnish with the fresh parsley, then
  serve.

Sun-dried tomato quiches
Add a handful of chopped sun-dried tomatoes to
the egg mixture before filling the pastry cases.

Cheese and mushroom empanadas

PREPARATION TIME: 15 minutes
COOKING TIME: 20 minutes
MAKES: 12

2 tbsp olive oil
1 small onion, finely chopped
6 mushrooms, diced finely
1 clove of garlic, crushed
50 g / 1 ¾ oz / ⅔ cup fresh breadcrumbs
100 g / 3 ½ oz / 1 cup Cheddar cheese, grated
1 tsp Dijon mustard
500 g / 1 lb 2 oz all-butter puff pastry
1 egg, beaten

- Preheat the oven to 230°C (210°C fan) / 450F / gas 8.
- Heat the oil in a frying pan and fry the onion, mushrooms and garlic for 5 minutes, stirring occasionally.
- Stir in the breadcrumbs, cheese and mustard and season to taste with salt and pepper, then remove from the heat.
- Roll out the pastry on a lightly floured surface and cut out 12 circles.
- Put a heaped teaspoon of the cheese mixture in the middle of each circle, then fold in half and seal with beaten egg.
- Crimp the edges, transfer the pastries to a baking tray and brush the tops with egg.
- Bake the empanadas for 15 minutes or until golden brown and cooked through.

Cheese and spinach empanadas
Roughly chop some spinach and add to the pan with the onion, mushrooms and garlic, before adding the remaining ingredients.

Hummus toasted sandwich

PREPARATION TIME: 15 minutes
SERVES: 4

8 slices wholemeal seeded bread
1 tub red pepper hummus
1 tub beetroot hummus
a handful of fresh baby spinach
4 cherry tomatoes, sliced
½ cucumber, sliced
1 Hass avocado, sliced

- Preheat the grill to its highest setting.
- Toast the bread under the grill on one side until golden brown.
- Turn the slices over and toast on the other side until they just start to brown.
- Top each piece with some hummus, a handful of spinach, some sliced tomatoes, cucumber and slices of avocado, then serve warm.

Tzatziki toasted sandwich
Replace the hummus with a layer of tzatziki for a delicious Greek-inspired alternative.

Vegetable lentil soup

PREPARATION TIME: **10 minutes**
COOKING TIME: **20–25 minutes**
SERVES: **4**

1 tbsp olive oil
2 cloves garlic, crushed
2 medium onions, peeled and chopped
2 leeks, chopped
4 medium carrots, chopped
1 litre / 1 pint 15 fl. oz / 4 cups vegetable stock
400 g / 14 oz / 2 ⅓ cups cooked brown lentils
mint leaves, to garnish

- Heat the oil in a saucepan and fry the garlic and onions until softened.
- Add the chopped leeks and carrots to the pan and cook for 2 minutes, then stir in the vegetable stock and cooked lentils and bring to the boil.
- Simmer for 10 minutes then season to taste with salt and pepper.
- Ladle the soup into 4 warm bowls and garnish with mint.

Pearl barley soup
Replace the lentils with equal parts of cooked pearl barley for a nutritious grain soup.

Watercress omelette

PREPARATION TIME: 1 minute
COOKING TIME: 4–5 minutes
SERVES: 1

3 large eggs
salt and freshly ground black pepper
2 tbsp flat-leaf parsley
1 tbsp butter
½ packet watercress, to serve

- Break the eggs into a jug with a pinch of salt and pepper. Beat them gently to break up the yolks. Stir in the parsley.
- Heat the butter in a non-stick frying pan until sizzling then pour in the eggs.
- Cook over a medium heat until the eggs start to set around the outside. Use a spatula to draw the sides of the omelette into the middle and tilt the pan to fill the gaps with more liquid egg.
- Repeat the process until the top of the omelette is just set. Serve with some fresh watercress on the side.

Omelette with ratatouille
This omelette is delicious served with ratatouille. Try a mixture of slow-cooked tomatoes, courgettes (zucchinis) and aubergine (eggplant) for a succulent side dish.

Scrambled egg on rye

PREPARATION TIME: 2 minutes
COOKING TIME: 5 minutes
SERVES: 4

8 large eggs
2 tbsp butter
50 g / 1 ¾ oz baby chard leaves
1 loaf of dark rye bread, sliced to desired thickness
freshly ground black pepper

- Gently beat the eggs to break up the yolks.
- Heat the butter in a non-stick frying pan until sizzling then pour in the eggs.
- Cook over a low heat, stirring constantly until the eggs scramble.
- Stir in half of the baby chard and divide the egg between the 4 servings of rye bread.
- Serve with extra chard leaves on the side and a sprinkling of black pepper.

Scrambled tofu on rye
Replace the butter with 2 tablespoons of olive oil and replace the eggs with 600 g / 1 lb 5 oz of firm tofu. Crumble the tofu into a pan and season to taste. Add 1 teaspoon of turmeric and 1 teaspoon of cumin seeds for spice.

Griddled courgette with yogurt

PREPARATION TIME: 10 minutes
COOKING TIME: 10 minutes
SERVES: 4

4 medium-sized courgettes (zucchinis), yellow and green
2 tbsp extra-virgin olive oil
1 clove garlic, crushed
½ lemon, juiced
fresh basil leaves, to garnish

FOR THE YOGURT DIP
200 g / 7 oz / ¾ cup Greek yogurt
fresh dill, roughly chopped
fresh mint, roughly chopped
freshly ground black pepper

- Slice the courgette lengthways and season well.
- Heat a griddle pan until smoking hot.
- Combine the oil, garlic and lemon juice, then drizzle over the courgette slices.
- Place the courgette slices in the griddle pan and cook for 4–5 minutes on each side.
- To make the yogurt dip, combine all the ingredients and spoon into a serving bowl.
- Serve with fresh basil leaves and enjoy hot or cold.

Tofu and spinach crêpes

PREPARATION TIME: 5 minutes
COOKING TIME: 30 minutes
SERVES: 4

2 tbsp olive oil
2 garlic cloves, crushed
1 onion, finely chopped
a handful of spinach, roughly chopped
50 g / 1 ¾ oz firm tofu, mashed with a fork
150 g / 5 oz / 1 cup chickpea (gram) flour
325 ml / 11 fl. oz / 1 ⅓ cups milk
1 lemon, halved
fresh basil, to garnish

- Heat 1 tablespoon of oil in a large frying pan and fry the garlic and onions for 2 minutes.
- Stir in the spinach and crumbled tofu, then season to taste. Once the spinach has wilted and the tofu is cooked through, remove the pan from the heat and set to one side.
- Sieve the flour into a bowl and make a well in the middle. Add the milk and a pinch of salt. Gradually incorporate all the flour from around the outside to make a batter.
- Heat the oil in a small frying pan. Add a small ladle of batter and swirl the pan to coat the bottom.
- When it starts to dry and curl up at the edges, turn the crêpe over with a spatula and cook the other side until golden brown. Transfer the crêpe to a plate and cover with a clean tea towel to keep warm.
- Repeat the process until all the batter has been used, keeping the finished crêpes warm under the tea towel.
- Divide the crêpes between 4 warm plates and add a generous amount of filling to each crêpe. Squeeze over the lemon.
- Garnish with some fresh basil leaves.

Spinach crêpes with lime pickle
Stir 3 tablespoons of lime pickle into the filling and divide the mixture between the 4 servings. This adds a zesty and irresistible spice that packs a punch.

Grilled mango and avocado tortilla

PREPARATION TIME: 5 minutes
COOKING TIME: 8 minutes
SERVES: 4

2 tbsp olive oil
1 red onion, sliced
2 cloves garlic, crushed
½ tsp chilli (chili) powder
1 punnet cherry tomatoes, halved
2 Hass avocado, pitted and sliced
1 ripe mango, pitted and sliced
1 lime, juiced
4 flour tortillas
a handful of fresh basil, to garnish

- Heat the oil in a pan then lightly fry the red onion and garlic with the chilli powder for 4 minutes.
- Add the tomatoes, avocado and mango and chargrill for 3–4 minutes. Then add the juice of half a lime.
- Divide the mixture between the 4 tortillas and season with salt and black pepper.
- Add a few leaves of basil and a splash of fresh lime juice. Serve immediately.

Grilled mango and avocado boats
For a wheat- and gluten-free option, replace the tortillas with romaine lettuce leaves and fill each leaf with the delicious mix.

Avocado cream bruschetta

PREPARATION TIME: **10 minutes**
SERVES: **6–8**

2 large Hass avocados
1 lime, juiced
1 tbsp extra-virgin olive oil
1 tsp chilli (chili) flakes, plus extra to garnish
fresh coriander (cilantro) leaves
1 pinch of sea salt
freshly ground black pepper
1 ciabatta, sliced
a handful of edible flowers, to garnish (optional)
flat-leaf parsley, to garnish

- Remove the stones from each avocado and scoop out the flesh.
- Add the avocado, lime, oil, chilli flakes, coriander, salt and pepper to a blender. Blitz until smooth. Add some water if necessary.
- Meanwhile, lightly grill the ciabatta slices on both sides until they start to turn golden.
- Spoon the avocado cream onto the ciabatta slices and garnish with some flowers, parsley and chilli flakes before serving.

Creamed potato and garlic soup

PREPARATION TIME: **5 minutes**
COOKING TIME: **30 minutes**
SERVES: **4**

2 tbsp olive oil, plus extra to drizzle
2 tbsp butter
1 onion, finely chopped
2 cloves garlic, crushed
2 medium potatoes, cubed
1 litre / 1 pint 15 fl. oz / 4 cups vegetable stock
1 teaspoon black peppercorns
1 pinch of dill

- Heat the oil and butter in a pan and fry the onion for 5 minutes.
- Add the garlic and potatoes to the pan and cook for 2 more minutes then stir in the vegetable stock and bring to the boil.
- Simmer for 15 minutes then blend until smooth with a liquidizer or hand blender.
- Serve with a drizzle of olive oil and a sprinkle of the peppercorns and dill.

Sweet potato and garlic soup
Replace the normal potatoes for the same quantity of sweet potatoes. The skins can be kept on or removed, but remember to scrub well first.

Mini tomato and feta tarts

PREPARATION TIME: 10 minutes
COOKING TIME: 15 minutes
MAKES: 4–6

3 eggs, beaten
100 g / 3 ½ oz feta, crumbled
250 g / 9 oz all-butter puff pastry
150 g / 5 oz cherry tomatoes
1 tbsp basil leaves, finely chopped
fresh oregano, to garnish

- Preheat the oven to 220°C (200°C fan) / 425F / gas 7.
- Beat the eggs in a mixing bowl. Add the crumbled feta and season to taste.
- Roll out the puff pastry on a floured surface and cut into circles.
- Transfer the pastry to a tart tray, or a muffin tray, and add the egg mixture, tomatoes and basil into each tart.
- Bake for 15 minutes or until the pastry is cooked and the tarts are golden.
- Garnish with oregano. Serve hot or cold.

Tomato and goat's cheese tarts
Replace the feta with the same amount of crumbled goat's cheese for a strong cheesy taste.

Grilled corn with garlic butter

PREPARATION TIME: 25 minutes
COOKING TIME: 16 minutes
SERVES: 4

100 g / 3 ½ oz / ½ cup butter, softened
1 clove garlic, crushed
1 tsp sea salt
4 sweetcorn cobs
2 sprigs rosemary, finely chopped
1 tsp salt flakes, to garnish

- Mix the butter with the garlic and season with salt and pepper. Shape into 4 small rounds and chill for 20 minutes.
- Meanwhile, bring a large saucepan of water to the boil, add salt and cook the sweetcorn cobs for 8 minutes. Drain well.
- Heat a griddle pan until smoking hot, then griddle the sweetcorn cobs for 8 minutes, turning occasionally.
- Serve with the butter rounds to coat the sweetcorn cobs. Sprinkle some rosemary and salt flakes on top to garnish.

Grilled corn with smoked paprika
Replace the rosemary with half a teaspoon of smoked paprika, which is delicious with the garlic butter.

Mushroom and parsley vol-au-vents

PREPARATION TIME: 15 minutes
COOKING TIME: 20 minutes
MAKES: 16

450 g / 1 lb all-butter puff pastry
1 egg, beaten
3 tbsp butter
2 onions, finely chopped
3 cloves garlic, crushed
100 g / 3 ½ oz / ⅔ cup mushrooms, sliced
1 tbsp plain (all-purpose) flour
300 ml / 10 fl. oz / 1 ¼ cups milk
parsley, finely chopped

- Preheat the oven to 220°C (200°C fan) / 425F / gas 7 and line a baking tray with greaseproof paper.
- Roll out the pastry on a floured surface and use a 7 cm (2 ¾ in) round pastry cutter to cut out 32 circles.
- Transfer 16 circles to a baking tray and remove the middles from the rest using a 4 cm (1 ½ in) cutter.
- Attach the 16 pastry rings to the 16 bases with a little beaten egg.
- Bake the pastry cases for 15–20 minutes.
- Meanwhile, heat half of the butter in a frying pan and lightly fry the onions and garlic. Add the mushrooms and cook for 5 minutes.
- Heat the rest of the butter in a saucepan and stir in the flour.
- Gradually add the milk and stir until the sauce thickens, then add the fried onions and mushrooms.
- Once the pastries are cooked, spoon in the mushroom mixture and sprinkle with some fresh parsley.

Vol-au-vents with crème fraiche
Replace the milk for the same quantity of crème fraiche for a creamier and richer taste.

Porcini and goat's cheese tart

PREPARATION TIME: 40 minutes
COOKING TIME: 35 minutes
SERVES: 4

3 eggs, lightly beaten
a small sprig of thyme
1 goat's cheese log, sliced
12 porcini mushrooms

FOR THE PASTRY
100 g / 3 ½ oz / ½ cup butter, cubed
200 g / 7 oz / 1 ⅓ cups plain (all-purpose) flour

- To make the pastry, rub the butter into the flour and add just enough cold water to bind.
- Chill for 30 minutes then roll out on a floured surface.
- Preheat the oven to 200°C (180°C fan) / 400F / gas 6.
- Line a medium-sized rectangular baking tray with pastry and prick with a fork. Then line the pastry with oven-safe cling film and fill with baking beans then bake for 10 minutes.
- Beat the eggs in a bowl and season. Add a little flour to thicken, then add a little thyme.
- Once the pastry is ready, pour in the egg mixture and arrange the goat's cheese slices on top.
- Lay the mushrooms on top and then garnish with the remaining thyme.
- Bake the tart for 25 minutes or until the pastry is golden brown and cooked through.

Porcini and Camembert tart
Replace the goat's cheese for the same amount of Camembert for a delicious alternative.

Leek, potato and rosemary soup

PREPARATION TIME: **5 minutes**
COOKING TIME: **30 minutes**
SERVES: **4**

2 tbsp olive oil
2 tbsp butter
3 leeks, halved and thickly sliced
2 cloves garlic, crushed
3 medium potatoes, cubed
1 litre / 1 pint 15 fl. oz / 4 cups vegetable stock
½ tsp dried rosemary

- Heat the oil and butter in a saucepan and fry the leeks for 8 minutes or until softened.
- Add the garlic and potatoes to the pan and cook for 2 more minutes, then stir in the vegetable stock and dried rosemary and bring to the boil.
- Simmer for 15–20 minutes then adjust the seasoning with salt and pepper.
- Once cooked, use a hand blender and blend the soup until smooth.
- Divide the soup between 4 serving bowls, then drizzle with a little extra-virgin olive oil.

Vegan leek and potato soup
Replace the butter with dairy-free butter for a vegan version, and serve with some fresh sourdough bread.

Spanish omelette tarts

PREPARATION TIME: **5 minutes**
COOKING TIME: **25 minutes**
MAKES: **4**

2 tbsp olive oil
1 small onion, finely chopped
1 red pepper, diced
3 large eggs
chives, to garnish

- Preheat the oven to 190°C (170°C fan) / 375F / gas 5.
- Heat the oil in a frying pan and fry the onion and pepper for 5 minutes or until softened.
- Gently whisk the eggs in a bowl until smoothly combined then stir in the vegetables and season generously with salt and pepper.
- Pour the egg mixture into individual cupcake moulds, then lower the oven temperature to 150°C (130°C fan) / 300F / gas 2 and bake for 20 minutes or until just set in the middle and golden on the outside.
- Serve with a garnish of chives.

Three-pepper egg tarts
Roughly chop half a red, green and yellow pepper and add to the egg mixture. You could also add a teaspoon of dried chilli (chili) flakes for a spicy kick.

Herbed cheese scones

PREPARATION TIME: **30 minutes**
COOKING TIME: **12–15 minutes**
MAKES: **10–12**

75 g / 2 ⅔ oz / ⅓ cup butter, cubed
250 g / 9 oz / 1 ⅔ cups self-raising flour, plus extra for dusting
½ tsp mustard powder
¼ tsp cayenne pepper
150 ml / 5 ⅓ fl. oz / ⅔ cup milk, plus extra for brushing
100 g / 3 ½ oz / ½ cup sun-dried tomatoes
a handful of fresh basil leaves
100 g / 3 ½ oz / 1 cup Red Leicester cheese, grated

- Preheat the oven to 220°C (200°C fan) / 425F / gas 7 and line a baking tray with greaseproof paper.
- Rub the butter into the flour with your fingertips until it resembles fine breadcrumbs then stir in the mustard powder and cayenne pepper.
- Add the milk, sun-dried tomatoes, basil and cheese and mix together into a dough.
- Turn the dough out onto a floured work surface and flatten it into a rectangle, 2 cm (¾ in) thick.
- Use a pastry cutter to stamp out the scones. Transfer to the baking tray, and brush with milk.
- Bake for 12–15 minutes until the scones have risen and are golden. Transfer the scones to a wire rack to cool a little before serving.

Cheese scones with cottage cheese
Serve the scones with a generous layer of cottage cheese mixed with chives.

Parmesan choux buns

PREPARATION TIME: **30 minutes**
COOKING TIME: **20 minutes**
MAKES: **16**

2 tbsp olive oil

55 g / 2 oz / ¼ cup butter, cubed

75 g / 2 ⅔ oz / ½ cup strong white bread flour, sieved

2 large eggs, beaten

50 g / 1 ¾ oz / ½ cup vegetarian Parmesan, finely grated

tomato preserves, to serve (optional)

- Preheat the oven to 200°C (180°C fan) / 400F / gas 6.
- Oil and line a large baking tray with greaseproof paper, then spray it with a little water.
- Put the butter in a saucepan with 150 ml / 5 ⅓ fl. oz / ⅔ cup water and heat until the butter melts and the water starts to boil.
- Turn off the heat and immediately beat in the flour with a wooden spoon until it forms a smooth ball of pastry.
- Stir in the egg a little at a time until you have a glossy paste, then beat in the Parmesan.
- Spoon the pastry into a piping bag fitted with a large star nozzle and pipe 2.5 cm (1 in) buns onto the baking tray.
- Bake for 10 minutes, then increase the heat to 220°C (200°C fan) / 425F / gas 7 and bake for another 10 minutes.
- Transfer the choux buns to a wire rack and make a small hole in the underneath of each one with a skewer so the steam can escape.
- Serve with some tomato preserves.

Cheddar choux buns
Replace the Parmesan for some grated Cheddar cheese and serve with a side of chutney.

Eggs and mushrooms on sourdough

PREPARATION TIME: **5 minutes**
COOKING TIME: **10–15 minutes**
SERVES: **4**

40 g / 1 ½ oz / ¼ cup butter

80 g / 3 oz / ½ cup button mushrooms, halved

6 eggs

4 thick slices white sourdough bread, toasted and buttered

4 tbsp guacamole

- Heat the butter in a pan and cook the mushrooms until golden and all the excess moisture has evaporated. Remove and set to one side.
- Crack the eggs into the pan and lightly fry. Ensure that the yolk is still runny.
- Slice the sourdough and add a spoonful of guacamole. Add the fried egg and some mushrooms.
- Add a pinch of salt and freshly ground black pepper. Serve immediately.

Rustic vegetable toast
Replace the guacamole for some wilted spinach and a grilled tomato for a more traditional take on the recipe.

Spring vegetable broth

PREPARATION TIME: **5 minutes**
COOKING TIME: **25 minutes**
SERVES: **4**

2 tbsp olive oil

1 white onion, finely chopped

2 medium potatoes, cubed

3 large carrots, cubed

150 g / 5 oz / 1 cup green beans

150 g / 5 oz / 1 cup peas, defrosted if frozen

1 litre / 1 pint 15 fl. oz / 4 cups vegetable stock

a few sprigs of parsley, to serve

- Heat the oil in a saucepan and fry the onions until softened.
- Add the vegetables to the pan and cook for 2 minutes, then stir in the vegetable stock and bring to the boil.
- Simmer for 10–15 minutes then season to taste.
- Ladle the soup into 4 warm bowls and garnish with parsley.

Spring onion broth
Replace the carrots and beans with a small bunch of chopped spring onions for a light onion alternative.

Mushroom and nutmeg soup

PREPARATION TIME: 5 minutes
COOKING TIME: 30 minutes
SERVES: 4

2 tbsp olive oil
2 tbsp butter
1 onion, finely chopped
400 g / 14 oz / 2 ⅔ cups mushrooms, chopped
2 cloves garlic, crushed
1 litre / 1 pint 15 fl. oz / 4 cups vegetable stock
100 ml / 3 ½ fl. oz / ½ cup double (heavy) cream
½ tsp freshly ground nutmeg

- Heat the oil and butter in a saucepan and fry the onion for 5 minutes or until softened.
- Finely slice 4 mushrooms and set to one side.
- Add the garlic and remaining mushrooms to the pan and cook for 5 minutes, then stir in the vegetable stock and bring to the boil.
- Simmer for 15 minutes then stir in the double cream and nutmeg.
- Blend the soup until smooth with a liquidizer or hand blender, according to the manufacturer's instructions, then taste the soup and adjust the seasoning as desired.
- Using the same pan, lightly sauté the sliced mushrooms with a little oil, salt and pepper.
- Ladle the soup into warm bowls and garnish with the sautéed mushrooms.

Mushroom and coconut soup
Replace the double cream with a 400ml / 14 fl. oz can of coconut milk for a lighter variation.

Creamy tomato and pesto soup

PREPARATION TIME: 5 minutes
COOKING TIME: 35 minutes
SERVES: 4

2 tbsp olive oil
1 onion, finely chopped
4 cloves garlic, crushed
450 g / 1 lb tomatoes, diced
500 ml / 17 ⅔ fl. oz / 2 cups vegetable stock
2 tbsp pesto, to garnish
double cream, to garnish
fresh basil leaves, to garnish

- Heat the oil in a saucepan and fry the onion for 8 minutes or until softened.
- Add the garlic to the pan and cook for 2 more minutes, then stir in the tomatoes and vegetable stock and bring to the boil.
- Simmer for 20 minutes then blend until smooth with a liquidizer or hand blender.
- Taste the soup and adjust the seasoning with salt and pepper.
- Ladle into bowls and stir in a little pesto and double cream.
- Garnish with a few fresh basil leaves then serve.

Sun-dried tomato and walnut soup
Replace the pesto and double cream for chopped walnuts and sun-dried tomatoes and a handful of rocket (arugula) leaves. Drizzle the soup with some extra-virgin olive oil and serve.

Tofu and parsley omelette

PREPARATION TIME: **1 minute**
COOKING TIME: **4–5 minutes**
SERVES: **1**

3 large eggs
2 tbsp flat-leaf parsley
50 g / 1 ¾ oz firm tofu, cubed
1 tbsp butter

Feta and parsley omelette
Replace the tofu for 35g / 1 ¼ oz of crumbled
feta cheese.

- Break the eggs into a jug with a pinch of salt and pepper and beat them gently to break up the yolks.
- Stir in the parsley and tofu.
- Heat the butter in a non-stick frying pan until sizzling then pour in the eggs.
- Cook over a medium heat until the eggs start to set around the outside. Use a spatula to draw the sides of the omelette into the middle and tilt the pan to fill the gaps with more liquid egg.
- Repeat the process until the top of the omelette is just set. Flip the omelette onto a plate and fold in half. Sprinkle over some more tofu and parsley to serve.

Pear, ricotta and honey toast

PREPARATION TIME: 5–8 minutes
SERVES: 4

4 slices wholemeal sultana bread, sliced
2 pears, cored and sliced
1 tub ricotta
a handful of fresh basil leaves, to garnish
a handful of walnuts and flaxseeds, to garnish
1 tbsp runny honey, to garnish

- Preheat the grill to its highest setting.
- Toast the bread under the grill on one side until golden brown.
- Turn the slices over and toast on the other side until they just start to turn golden.
- Then, top each piece with some pear, ricotta, basil, walnuts and flaxseeds.
- Drizzle with honey at the table.

Apricot and ricotta toast
Replace the pear with some lightly grilled (or uncooked) apricot slices. This is a deliciously sweet alternative that nicely complements the ricotta.

Mixed seed and goji scones

PREPARATION TIME: 10 minutes
COOKING TIME: 12–15 minutes
MAKES: 12

75 g / 2 ⅔ oz / ⅓ cup butter, cubed

150 g / 5 oz / 1 cup self-raising flour, plus extra for dusting

100 g / 3 ½ oz / ⅔ cup wholemeal flour

150 ml / 5 ⅓ fl. oz / ⅔ cup milk, plus extra for brushing

4 tbsp runny honey

4 tbsp flaxseeds

4 tbsp sunflower seeds

2 tbsp goji berries

- Preheat the oven to 220°C (200°C fan) / 425F / gas 7 and line a baking tray with greaseproof paper.
- Rub the butter into the flours with your fingertips until the mixture resembles fine breadcrumbs.
- Pour in the milk and honey and mix together into a dough.
- Turn the dough out onto a floured work surface and press it out into a rectangle, 2 cm (¾ in) thick.
- Use a 8 cm (3 in) round pastry cutter to cut out the scones and transfer them to the baking tray.
- Brush the scones with milk and sprinkle with the seeds and goji berries then bake for 12–15 minutes or until fully cooked through.
- Transfer the scones to a wire rack to cool a little before serving.

Vegan goji scones
Replace the butter with the same amount of dairy-free butter and replace the milk with a dairy-free milk, such as soya, almond or oat milk.

Peach and ricotta toast

PREPARATION TIME: 5 minutes
COOKING TIME: 8–10 minutes
SERVES: 4

4 slices baguette
4 tbsp ricotta
2 ripe peaches, stoned and sliced
2 tsp thyme leaves

- Preheat the grill to its highest setting.
- Cut the baguette into slices.
- Toast the bread under the grill on one side until golden brown.
- Turn the slices over and toast on the other side until they just start to crisp up.
- Top each piece with some ricotta, 3 slices of peach and sprinkle with thyme.

Peach and feta toast
Replace the ricotta with crumbled feta for a delicious salty and sweet alternative.

Apricot cooler

PREPARATION TIME: 2 minutes
COOKING TIME: 12–15 minutes
SERVES: 4

20 apricots, peeled, stoned and sliced
50 g / 1 ¾ oz / ¼ cup caster (superfine) sugar
100 ml / 3 ½ fl. oz / ½ cup white grape juice
a few sprigs mint, to garnish

- Put the apricots and sugar in a saucepan with the grape juice.
- Put a lid on the pan then simmer over a gentle heat for 8 minutes or until the apricots are tender but still hold their shape.
- Remove the lid and cook, stirring occasionally, until the liquid evaporates and the apricots are really soft.
- Chill in the fridge until cold, then garnish with some sprigs of mint.

Peach and lemon verbena cooler
Follow the same method above, but instead use peaches and some fresh lemon verbena to garnish.

Blueberry and strawberry granola

PREPARATION TIME: 5 minutes
COOKING TIME: 1 hour
SERVES: 6

75 ml / 2 ⅔ fl. oz / ⅓ cup maple syrup
75 ml / 2 ⅔ fl. oz / ⅓ cup apple juice
1 tbsp coconut oil
175 g / 6 oz / 1 ¾ cups rolled oats
50 g / 1 ¾ oz / ½ cup almonds
600 ml / 1 pint 2 fl. oz / 2 ½ cups coconut yogurt, to serve
a handful of fresh blueberries
a handful of fresh strawberries, sliced

- Preheat the oven to 160°C (140°C fan) / 325F / gas 3.
- Stir the maple syrup, apple juice and oil together in a bowl with a pinch of salt then toss it with the oats and almonds.
- Spread the mixture out on a large baking tray and bake for 1 hour, stirring every 10 minutes to ensure it all toasts evenly.
- Leave the granola to cool completely, then set to one side.
- Divide the coconut yogurt between 6 serving bowls and stir in the granola and fresh berries.

Superfood granola
Replace the coconut yogurt with milk and add some dried mulberries and goji berries for a super berry kick.

Traditional hot cross buns

PREPARATION TIME: 3 hours, 15 minutes
COOKING TIME: 15–20 minutes
MAKES: 12

55 g / 2 oz / ¼ cup butter, cubed

400 g / 14 oz / 2 ⅔ cups strong white bread flour, plus extra for dusting

½ tsp easy-blend dried yeast

4 tbsp caster (superfine) sugar

1 tsp fine sea salt

2 tsp mixed spice

100 g / 3 ½ oz / ½ cup mixed dried fruit

280 ml / 9 ¾ fl. oz / 1 cup warm water

4 tbsp plain (all-purpose) flour

1 egg, beaten

softened butter, for spreading

- Rub the butter into the bread flour and stir in the yeast, sugar, salt and spice. Add the dried fruit to the warm water and stir it into the dry ingredients.
- Knead the mixture on a lightly oiled surface for around 10 minutes, until the dough is smooth and elastic.
- Leave the dough to rest, covered with the mixing bowl, for 1–2 hours, until doubled in size.
- Shape the dough into 12 buns. Transfer to a greased baking tray, cover and leave to prove for 45 minutes.
- Preheat the oven to 220°C (200°C fan) / 425F / gas 7.
- Mix the plain flour with just enough water to make a thick paste. Spoon it into a piping bag.
- Brush the buns with egg and pipe a cross on top of each bun.
- Bake the buns for 15–20 minutes or until golden brown.
- Leave to cool on a wire rack then split in half and sandwich back together with butter.

Cranberry and orange buns
Replace the mixed dried fruit with the same amount of dried cranberries. Add the zest of 1 orange to the dough for a hint of orange.

Stewed apple and apricot crêpes

PREPARATION TIME: 10 minutes
COOKING TIME: 20–25 minutes
SERVES: 4

150 g / 5 oz / 1 cup plain (all-purpose) flour
325 ml / 11 fl. oz / 1⅓ cups whole milk
1 large egg, beaten
2 tbsp butter

FOR THE FILLING
125 g / 4⅓ oz / ⅔ cup dried apricots
4 Granny Smith apples, cored and sliced
1 cinnamon stick
600 ml / 1 pint 2 fl. oz / 2½ cups apple juice

Stewed apple and prune crêpes
Following the same method above, swap the dried apricots
for the same quantity of dried prunes (stones removed).

- For the filling, put the fruit and cinnamon in a saucepan and pour over the apple juice. Simmer for 5 minutes then turn off the heat.
- Put the oven on a low setting.
- Sieve the flour into a bowl and make a well in the middle. Pour in the milk and egg then use a whisk to incorporate all the flour from around the outside.
- Melt the butter in a small non-stick frying pan then whisk it into the batter.
- Put the buttered frying pan back over a low heat. Add a small ladle of batter and swirl the pan to coat the bottom.
- When it starts to dry and curl up at the edges, turn the crêpe over with a spatula and cook the other side until golden brown and cooked through.
- Transfer the crêpe to a plate, cover with a clean tea towel and keep warm in the oven.
- Repeat the process until all the batter has been used, then divide between 4 warm plates and spoon over the stewed fruit and serve as stacked wraps.

Almond granola with yogurt

PREPARATION TIME: 5 minutes
SERVES: 6

600 g / 1 lb 5 oz / 2 ½ cups coconut yogurt
200 g / 7 oz / 1 ⅓ cups black seedless grapes, halved
100 g / 3 ½ oz / ¾ cup whole almonds
100 g / 3 ½ oz / ½ cup dried cranberries
200 g / 7 oz / 2 cups ready-made granola
6 tbsp maple syrup

- Divide the coconut yogurt, grapes, almonds, cranberries and granola equally between the 6 bowls.
- Drizzle 1 tablespoon of maple syrup over the granola and yogurt, and serve.

Date and walnut granola
Replace the almonds and cranberries with the same quantities of dates (stones removed) and roughly chopped walnuts.

Strawberry and coconut yogurt pots

PREPARATION TIME: 5 minutes
SERVES: 4

4 tbsp strawberry jam
400 g / 14 oz / 1 ⅔ cups coconut yogurt
4 tbsp runny honey
200 g / 7 oz / 1 ⅓ cups strawberries, sliced
2 tbsp mint leaves, shredded

- Spoon half a tablespoon of strawberry jam into the bottom of each glass.
- Mix the yogurt with the honey and divide between the 4 glasses, layering with the sliced strawberries.
- Top with the remaining strawberries and jam, then sprinkle with shredded mint.

Coconut, cacao and raspberry yogurt
Replace the strawberry jam and fresh strawberries with the same amount of raspberry jam and fresh raspberries. Sprinkle with some cacao nibs before serving.

Vegan granola pots

PREPARATION TIME: **5 minutes**
SERVES: **8**

450 ml / 16 fl. oz / 1 ¾ cups coconut yogurt
150 g / 5 oz / 1 cup strawberries, sliced
150 g / 5 oz / 1 ½ cup granola

- Layer the yogurt, strawberries and granola in individual ramekins. Ensure a thick layer of yogurt is used so that the ingredients do not combine and mix together.
- Refrigerate until ready to serve.

Coconut yogurt with cacao nibs
Sprinkle 1 tablespoon of cacao nibs on top of the yogurt for a delicious crunch.

Strawberry jam croissants

PREPARATION TIME: **4 hours**
COOKING TIME: **30 minutes**
MAKES: **8**

350 g / 12 oz / 2 ⅓ cups strong white bread flour
1 tsp easy-blend yeast
75 ml / 2 ⅔ fl. oz / ⅓ cup warm water
2 large eggs, separated
75 ml / 2 ⅔ fl. oz / ⅓ cup semi-skimmed milk
50 ml / 1 ¾ fl. oz / ¼ cup double (heavy) cream
2 tbsp caster (superfine) sugar,
plus extra for dusting
1 tsp salt
250 g / 9 oz / 1 ¼ cups butter, chilled and cubed
8 tbsp strawberry jam

- Mix 50 g / 1 ¾ oz / ⅓ cup of the flour with the yeast and warm water and leave somewhere warm for 1 hour.
- Then whisk the egg yolks with the milk, cream, sugar and salt, then slowly incorporate it into the yeast mixture.
- Mix in the butter cubes and remaining flour, then knead briefly on a floured surface.
- Roll out the dough, then fold into thirds and roll again. Fold it into thirds then chill for 30 minutes.
- Repeat the rolling, folding and chilling twice more.
- Roll the dough into a square, cut into quarters and cut each one diagonally into 2 triangles.
- Roll into croissant shapes, adding 1 tablespoon of strawberry jam in the middle of each, then transfer them to a lined baking tray. Cover the croissants with oiled cling film and leave to rise for 1 hour.
- Preheat the oven to 200°C (180°C fan) / 400F / gas 6.
- Brush the croissants with egg white and bake for 30 minutes, reducing the heat to 180°C (160°C fan) / 350F / gas 4 after the first 10 minutes.
- Serve hot or cold.

Gooseberry jam croissants
Replace the strawberry jam with the same amount of gooseberry jam for a more unusual take on this classic continental breakfast.

Coffee and cacao smoothie

PREPARATION TIME: **10 minutes**
MAKES: **4**

400 ml / 14 fl. oz / 1 ⅔ cups almond milk
4 bananas, chopped
2 tbsp almond butter
1 tbsp espresso powder
1 tbsp cacao powder
4 dates, stones removed
a handful of ice

- Blend the almond milk, banana, almond butter, espresso powder, cacao powder, dates and a handful of ice.
- Serve cold.

Coffee and cacao nib smoothie
Sprinkle with 1 tablespoon of cacao nibs for added crunch.

Summer fruit salad

PREPARATION TIME: **10–15 minutes**
SERVES: **4**

4 small honeydew melons, cubed
100 g / 3 ½ oz nectarines
200 g / 7 oz / 1 ⅓ cups seedless green grapes
100 g / 3 ½ oz / ⅔ cup blueberries
100 g / 3 ½ oz / ⅔ cup raspberries
100 g / 3 ½ oz / ⅔ cup blackberries
fresh mint leaves, to garnish

- Using a sharp knife, cut the tops off the melons.
- Scoop out and discard the seeds, then use a melon baller to remove some of the flesh. Cut the rest of the flesh into large cubes and transfer to a bowl.
- Wash the nectarines, remove the stones and cut into cubes.
- Wash the grapes and berries and mix everything carefully together, then divide the fruit between 4 bowls.
- Garnish with sprigs of mint before serving.

Apple berry salad
Replace the grapes and melon with 4 Golden Delicious apples, cores removed and cut into generous chunks.

Apple and cinnamon buns

PREPARATION TIME: 3 hours, 30 minutes
COOKING TIME: 35 minutes
MAKES: 12

400 g / 14 oz / 2 ⅔ cups strong white bread flour
½ tsp easy-blend dried yeast
4 tbsp caster (superfine) sugar
1 tsp fine sea salt
1 tbsp ground cinnamon
1 tbsp coconut oil, melted
280 ml / 9 ¾ fl. oz / 1 cup warm water
75 g / 2 ⅔ oz / ½ cup dark brown sugar
2 tbsp butter, softened
1 eating apple, peeled and grated
1 egg, beaten
icing, to drizzle (optional)

- Combine flour, yeast, caster sugar, salt and half a tablespoon of cinnamon. Stir the oil into the water then stir into the dry ingredients.
- Knead the dough on an oiled surface until smooth.
- Leave the dough to rest in a lightly oiled bowl, covered with cling film, for 1–2 hours.
- Knead the dough for 2 minutes, then roll into a rectangle.
- Cream the brown sugar and butter together and stir in the apple.
- Spread the mixture over the dough and roll it up tightly.
- Cut into 12 slices and arrange in a 23 cm (9 in) round cake tin.
- Cover the rolls with oiled cling film and leave to prove for 1 hour or until doubled in size.
- Preheat the oven to 220°C (200°C fan) / 425F / gas 7.
- Brush the rolls with egg then transfer the tray to the top shelf of the oven and bake for 35 minutes.
- Leave to cool before drizzling over some icing and the remaining cinnamon.

Cinnamon and hazelnut rolls
Replace the apple with 50 g / 1 ¾ oz / ½ cup of chopped hazelnuts (cob nuts) and stir in with the brown sugar and butter.

Matcha tea smoothie

PREPARATION TIME: **5–10 minutes**
SERVES: **4**

400 ml / 14 fl. oz / 1 ⅔ cups almond milk
1 banana
1 Hass avocado
2 tbsp almond butter
a handful of spinach leaves, washed
2 tsp matcha powder
a handful of ice

- Blend the milk, banana, avocado, almond butter, spinach leaves, matcha powder and a handful of ice in a blender, according to the manufacturer's instructions.
- Serve cold.

Spirulina smoothie
Replace the matcha powder with the same amount of spirulina for a protein-rich alternative.

Iced blackberry and pomegranate smoothie

PREPARATION TIME: **5–10 minutes**
SERVES: **2**

200 g / 7 oz / 1 ⅓ cups frozen blackberries
150 ml / 5 ⅓ fl. oz / ⅔ cup pomegranate juice
a handful of ice
1 tbsp agave nectar
a sprig of mint

- Blend the frozen blackberries, pomegranate juice, ice and agave nectar in a blender, according to the manufacturer's instructions.
- Serve immediately with a sprig of mint.

Iced blackberry and coconut smoothie
Replace the pomegranate juice with the same amount of coconut water for a good thirst quencher.

Coconut and blueberry pancakes

PREPARATION TIME: 10 minutes
COOKING TIME: 25–30 minutes
MAKES: 12–16

250 g / 9 oz / 1 ⅔ cups plain (all-purpose) flour
2 tsp baking powder
2 large eggs
300 ml / 10 fl. oz / 1 ¼ cups coconut milk
2 tbsp melted coconut oil
2 tbsp shredded coconut, plus extra to serve
a handful of fresh blueberries
2 tbsp icing (confectioners') sugar, to serve
honey, to serve

- Mix the flour and baking powder in a bowl and make a well in the middle.
- Break in the eggs and pour in the coconut milk then use a whisk to gradually incorporate all the flour from around the outside.
- Melt the oil in a small frying pan then whisk it into the batter with the shredded coconut.
- Put the oiled frying pan back over a low heat. You will need a tablespoon of batter for each pancake and you should be able to cook 4 pancakes at a time in the frying pan.
- Spoon the batter into the pan and cook for 2 minutes or until small bubbles start to appear on the surface.
- Turn the pancakes over with a spatula and cook the other side until golden brown and cooked through.
- Repeat until all the batter has been used, keeping the finished batches warm in a low oven.
- Pile the pancakes onto warm plates and sprinkle with some more shredded coconut, some blueberries and the icing sugar.
- Serve with honey on the side to be drizzled over the pancakes as desired.

Chia and coconut pancakes
Add 2 tablespoons of chia seeds to the batter and follow the method as above.

Summer berry pancakes

PREPARATION TIME: **10 minutes**
COOKING TIME: **25–30 minutes**
MAKES: **12–16**

250 g / 9 oz / 1 ⅔ cups plain (all-purpose) flour
2 tsp baking powder
2 large eggs
300 ml / 10 fl. oz / 1 ¼ cups milk
2 tbsp melted butter
450 g / 1 lb / 3 cups mixed berries, to serve
maple syrup, to serve

- Mix the flour and baking powder in a bowl and make a well in the middle.
- Break in the eggs and pour in the milk. Use a whisk to incorporate all the flour from around the outside of the bowl.
- Melt the butter in a frying pan then whisk into the batter.
- Put the buttered frying pan back over a low heat. You will need a tablespoon of batter for each pancake and you should be able to cook 4 pancakes at a time.
- Spoon the batter into the pan and cook for 2 minutes.
- Turn the pancakes over with a spatula and cook the other side until golden brown and cooked through.
- Repeat until all the batter has been used.
- Pile the pancakes onto warm plates. Serve with a handful of mixed berries and a drizzle of maple syrup.

Lemon and cardamom pancakes
For an irresistible and unusual alternative, add the zest of a lemon and some cardamom. Remove the cardamom pods and finely chop the seeds or use a pestle and mortar for the best results. Add to the pancake mix and cook as above.

Fruity chia yogurt bowl

PREPARATION TIME: **10 minutes**
MAKES: **4**

400 g / 14 oz / 1 ⅔ cups Greek yogurt
2 large ripe mangoes, peeled, stoned and cubed
4 kiwi fruits, peeled and sliced
4 tbsp desiccated coconut
4 tsp chia seeds

* Divide the Greek yogurt between 4 small bowls.
* Add the chopped mango and kiwi pieces and then sprinkle the coconut and chia seeds on top.
* Serve immediately.

Pineapple and coconut yogurt bowl
Replace the mango with pineapple pieces and the Greek yogurt with coconut yogurt for a delicious alternative.

Summer berry French toast

PREPARATION TIME: **4 minutes**
COOKING TIME: **4 minutes**
SERVES: **4**

2 large eggs
75 ml / 2 ⅔ fl. oz / ⅓ cup semi-skimmed milk
2 tbsp butter
4 slices thick white bread
2 tbsp icing (confectioners') sugar
fresh strawberries, blueberries and mint leaves, to serve

* Lightly beat the eggs with the milk in a wide, shallow dish and heat the butter in a large frying pan until sizzling.
* Cut the bread slices in half and dip each slice in the egg mixture on both sides until coated.
* Fry them in the butter for 2 minutes on each side.
* Sprinkle the icing sugar over the French toast then serve with the strawberries, blueberries and mint leaves.

Cinnamon and raisin French toast
Add 100 g / 3 ½ oz / ½ cup finely chopped raisins and 1 teaspoon of ground cinnamon to the egg mixture for a sweet and comforting take on this classic breakfast treat.

Super green goji smoothie

PREPARATION TIME: **5–10 minutes**
SERVES: **2**

200 g / 7 oz fresh or frozen spinach
2 kiwi fruits, skin removed and roughly chopped
1 Hass avocado, skin removed and roughly chopped
2 tbsp chia seeds
250 ml / 9 fl. oz / 1 cup coconut water
a handful of ice
a handful of fresh mint leaves
1 tbsp goji berries, to garnish

- Add all the ingredients except the goji berries to the blender. Blend until smooth, according to the manufacturer's instructions.
- Serve cold with the goji berries on top.

Strawberry and blackberry granola

PREPARATION TIME: **5–10 minutes**
SERVES: **4**

200 g / 7 oz / 2 cups ready-made granola
250 g / 9 oz / 1 ⅔ cups strawberries, sliced
250 g / 9 oz / 1 ⅔ cups blackberries
milk, to serve
mint leaves, to garnish

- Divide the granola, strawberries and blackberries equally between the 4 bowls.
- Add preferred quantity of milk and garnish with the mint leaves then serve.

Super green coconut smoothie
Replace the coconut water with the same amount of coconut milk for a creamier consistency.

Choc-chip granola
For a naughty and decadent variation, simply add 100 g / 3 ½ oz / ⅔ cup chocolate chips to the granola and divide between the 4 bowls. Top with the berries and serve with milk or yogurt.

THE
COOKERY
COLLECTION

Granola berry pots

PREPARATION TIME: 5 minutes
COOKING TIME: 1 hour
SERVES: 6

75 ml / 2 ⅔ fl. oz / ⅓ cup maple syrup
75 ml / 2 ⅔ fl. oz / ⅓ cup apple juice
1 tbsp coconut oil
175 g / 6 oz / 1 ¾ cups rolled oats
50 g / 1 ¾ oz / ½ cup walnuts
50 g / 1 ¾ oz / ½ cup mixed seeds
50 g / 1 ¾ oz / ¼ cup raisins
600 ml / 1 pint 2 fl. oz / 2 ½ cups coconut yogurt
a handful of fresh mixed berries

- Preheat the oven to 160°C (140°C fan) / 325F / gas 3.
- Stir the maple syrup, apple juice and oil together in a bowl with a pinch of salt then toss it with the oats, walnuts and seeds.
- Spread the mixture out evenly on a large baking tray and bake for 1 hour, stirring every 10 minutes to ensure the mixture toasts evenly.
- Leave the granola to cool completely, then stir in the raisins.
- Divide the coconut yogurt between 6 jars and stir in the granola and fresh berries.

Very berry granola
Replace the coconut yogurt with milk and add some freeze-dried raspberries and strawberries for a mixed berry kick.

Banana breakfast smoothie

PREPARATION TIME: 5–10 minutes
SERVES: 4

400 ml / 14 fl. oz / 1 ⅔ cups almond milk
4 bananas, chopped
2 tbsp almond butter
1 tbsp maca powder
4 dates, stones removed
a handful of ice
ready-made granola, to garnish

- Whizz the milk, banana, almond butter, maca powder, dates and a handful of ice in a blender, according to the manufacturer's instructions.
- Garnish with the granola and serve cold.

Peanut butter and banana smoothie
Replace the almond butter with the same amount of peanut butter for a delicious variation. Garnish with the granola and some roughly chopped peanuts.

Cacao, banana and chia breakfast pot

PREPARATION TIME: **10 minutes**
SERVES: **2**

600 ml / 1 pint 2 fl. oz / 2 ½ cups coconut yogurt
75 ml / 2 ⅔ fl. oz / ⅓ cup maple syrup
2 tbsp cacao powder
a pinch of salt
2 bananas, mashed
a pinch of cinnamon
2 tbsp chia seeds, plus extra to garnish
50 g / 1 ¾ oz / ½ cup ready-made granola
½ banana, sliced
2 tsp flaked dark chocolate, if desired

- Combine the coconut yogurt with the maple syrup, cacao powder and a pinch of salt.
- Mix in the remaining mashed banana with a pinch of cinnamon and the chia seeds.
- Divide the granola between the two glasses, then distribute the mixture on top.
- Sprinkle some sliced banana on top, with additional chia seeds and flaked dark chocolate if desired. Serve immediately.

Cacao, berry and chia breakfast pot
Replace the mashed banana .with some frozen berries, and the sliced banana with a handful of fresh berries.

Acai chia smoothie bowl

PREPARATION TIME: 10 minutes
SERVES: 4

400 g / 14 oz / 1 ⅔ cups coconut yogurt
a handful of frozen berries
1 tbsp acai powder
2 tbsp desiccated coconut
4 tsp chia seeds
1 tbsp pumpkin seeds
a handful of fresh blueberries and raspberries, washed
chopped almonds, to garnish
apple slices, to garnish

- Blend the coconut yogurt with the frozen berries and acai powder.
- Divide the yogurt between 4 bowls and sprinkle the coconut and chia seeds on top.
- Garnish with the seeds, berries, almonds and apple slices.

Green chia smoothie bowl
Blitz a handful of spinach leaves with the yogurt and a tablespoon of wheatgrass for a super green, fibre-rich start to the day.

Black Forest smoothie

PREPARATION TIME: 5–10 minutes
SERVES: 4

400 ml / 14 fl. oz / 1 ⅔ cups milk
2 bananas, chopped
a handful of frozen blackberries
a handful of frozen cherries
4 dates, stones removed
a handful of ice

- Blend the milk, banana, frozen berries and cherries, dates and a handful of ice in a blender, according to the manufacturer's instructions.
- Serve cold.

Superfood smoothie
Add 1 tablespoon of acai powder and a handful of goji berries for a superfood kick.

Almond and lemon muffins

PREPARATION TIME: 10 minutes
COOKING TIME: 20–25 minutes
MAKES: 12

1 large egg
120 ml / 4 fl. oz / ½ cup coconut oil, melted
120 ml / 4 fl. oz / ½ cup milk
375 g / 13 oz / 2 ½ cups self-raising flour, sifted
1 tsp baking powder
200 g / 7 oz / ¾ cup caster (superfine) sugar
50 g / 1 ¾ oz / ½ cup ground almonds
1 lemon, juiced and zested

- Preheat the oven to 180°C (160°C fan) / 350F / gas 4 and oil a 12-hole silicone muffin mould.
- Beat the egg in a jug with the oil and milk until well mixed.
- Mix together the flour, baking powder, sugar and the almonds then pour in the egg mixture and stir just enough to combine.
- Spoon the mixture into the mould, then bake for 20–25 minutes.
- Test with a wooden toothpick, if it comes out clean, the muffins are done.
- Transfer the muffins to a wire rack and leave to cool completely.
- Top the muffins with some lemon juice and zest, then serve.

Orange and almond muffins
Replace the lemon juice and zest with the juice and zest of 1 medium-sized orange.

Maple and apple pancakes

PREPARATION TIME: 10 minutes
COOKING TIME: 30 minutes
MAKES: 12–16

2 apples, peeled, cored and finely sliced
250 ml / 9 fl. oz / 1 cup maple syrup
250 g / 9 oz / 1 ⅔ cups plain (all-purpose) flour
2 tsp baking powder
2 large eggs
300 ml / 10 fl. oz / 1 ¼ cups semi-skimmed milk
2 tbsp butter
Greek yogurt, to serve

- Put the apple slices in a small saucepan with the maple syrup and simmer gently for 4 minutes.
- Mix the flour and baking powder in a bowl and make a well in the middle.
- Break in the eggs and pour in the milk then use a whisk to gradually incorporate all the flour from round the outside.
- Melt the butter in a small frying pan then whisk it into the batter.
- Put the buttered frying pan back over a low heat. You will need a tablespoon of batter for each pancake and you should be able to cook 4 pancakes at a time in the frying pan.
- Spoon the batter into the pan and cook for 2 minutes or until small bubbles start to appear on the surface.
- Turn the pancakes over with a spatula and cook the other side until cooked through.
- Repeat until all the batter has been used, keeping the finished batches warm in a low oven.
- Stack the pancakes, layering with the maple apples as you go.
- Drizzle with a little maple syrup and serve with a side of Greek yogurt.

Cinnamon and pear pancakes
Replace the apples with pears. Slice 2 pears leaving the skins on, and simmer gently in a pan with the maple syrup. Add 1 teaspoon of ground cinnamon to the maple and pear mixture for a warming spice.

Energy boost juice

PREPARATION TIME: 5–10 minutes
SERVES: 4

400 ml / 14 fl. oz / 1 ⅔ cups coconut water
a handful of frozen raspberries and strawberries
200 ml / 6 ¾ fl. oz / ¾ cup fresh pomegranate juice
200 ml / 6 ¾ fl. oz / ¾ cup fresh beetroot juice
a handful of ice

- Blend the coconut water, frozen berries, pomegranate and beetroot juice with a handful of ice in a blender, according to the manufacturer's instructions.
- Serve cold.

Protein pick-me-up juice
Add a teaspoon of spirulina to the energy juice mix before blending for an extra protein pick-me-up.

Orange and chia yogurt

PREPARATION TIME: 10 minutes
SERVES: 4

400 g / 14 oz / 1 ⅔ cups Greek yogurt
4 tbsp runny honey
4 tbsp chia seeds
100 g / 7 oz / 1 cup muesli
2 oranges, peeled and chopped

- Mix the yogurt with the honey and chia seeds.
- Divide the yogurt between the 4 glasses and layer with the muesli.
- Top each glass with some orange pieces and a little more yogurt.
- Serve chilled.

Grapefruit and chia yogurt
Replace the orange pieces with the same amount of pink grapefruit pieces for a zingy start to the day.

THE COOKERY COLLECTION

Nutty kiwi porridge

PREPARATION TIME: 2 minutes
COOKING TIME: 4–5 minutes
SERVES: 4

600 ml / 1 pint 2 fl. oz / 2 ½ cups milk, plus extra to serve
125 g / 4 ⅓ oz / 1 ¼ cups rolled oats
½ tsp ground cinnamon
4 tbsp runny honey, plus extra to serve
2 kiwi fruits, peeled and chopped
a handful of roasted pecans and almonds, chopped

- Mix the milk with the oats and cinnamon. Stir the mixture over a medium heat until it starts to simmer.
- Add the honey and a pinch of salt then reduce the heat to its lowest setting and continue to stir for 4–5 minutes.
- Divide the porridge between 4 bowls and top with the chopped kiwi fruit and nuts.
- Drizzle honey over the top as desired.

Nut and date porridge
Replace the kiwi fruit with some chopped dates for a delicious chewy texture and toffee-like taste.

Strawberry Bircher muesli

PREPARATION TIME: **Overnight**
SERVES: **4**

200 g / 7 oz / 1 ⅓ cups strawberries, sliced
400 g / 14 oz / 1 ⅔ cups Greek yogurt
100 g / 3 ½ oz / 1 cup rolled oats
4 tbsp runny honey
2 tbsp mint leaves

- Line each glass with a few strawberry slices.
- Mix the yogurt with the oats and honey. Divide between the 4 glasses.
- Leave the glasses covered in the fridge overnight, allowing the oats to soften.
- When ready to serve, top with the strawberries and garnish with the mint leaves.

Coconut and strawberry Bircher muesli
Replace the Greek yogurt with coconut yogurt for a satisfying alternative. Garnish with desiccated coconut instead of the mint leaves.

American pancakes with chopped nuts

PREPARATION TIME: **10 minutes**
COOKING TIME: **30 minutes**
MAKES: **12–16**

250 g / 9 oz / 1 ⅔ cups plain (all-purpose) flour
2 tsp baking powder
2 large eggs
300 ml / 10 fl. oz / 1 ¼ cups milk
2 tbsp melted butter
chopped walnuts, to serve
chopped pecans, to serve
1 sliced banana, to serve
4 tbsp maple syrup, to serve

- Mix the flour and baking powder in a bowl and make a well in the middle.
- Break in the eggs and pour in the milk then use a whisk to incorporate all the flour from round the outside.
- Melt the butter in a frying pan then whisk into the batter.
- Put the buttered frying pan back over a low heat. You will need a tablespoon of batter for each pancake and you should be able to cook 4 pancakes at a time.
- Spoon the batter into the pan and cook for 2 minutes. Turn the pancakes over with a spatula and cook the other side until golden brown and cooked through. Repeat until all the batter has been used.
- Pile the pancakes onto warm plates and top each one with the chopped walnuts, chopped pecans and banana slices. Drizzle 1 tablespoon of maple syrup over each pancake stack.
- Serve immediately, while warm.

American raisin pancake stack
Mix 200 g / 7 oz / 1 cup raisins into the pancake batter for a chewy texture.

Chocolate orange croissants

PREPARATION TIME: 4 hours
COOKING TIME: 30 minutes
MAKES: 8

350 g / 12 oz / 2 ⅓ cups strong white bread flour

1 tsp easy-blend yeast

75 ml / 2 ⅔ fl. oz / ⅓ cup warm water

2 large eggs, separated

75 ml / 2 ⅔ fl. oz / ⅓ cup milk

50 ml / 1 ¾ fl. oz / ¼ cup double (heavy) cream

2 tbsp caster (superfine) sugar, plus extra for dusting

1 tsp salt

250 g / 9 oz / 1 ¼ cups butter, chilled and cubed

200 g / 7 oz orange-flavoured plain chocolate, chopped

2 tbsp orange-flavoured chocolate, melted, to drizzle

Lemon chocolate croissants
Replace the orange-flavoured chocolate with the
same amount of lemon-flavoured plain chocolate for
a decadent alternative.

- Mix 50 g / 1 ¾ oz / ⅓ cup of the flour with the yeast and
  the water and leave somewhere warm for 1 hour.
- Whisk the egg yolks with the milk, cream, sugar and salt,
  then slowly incorporate it into the yeast mixture.
- Mix in the butter cubes and remaining flour, then knead
  briefly on a floured surface.
- Roll out the dough, then fold into thirds and roll again.
  Fold it into thirds then chill for 30 minutes.
- Repeat the rolling, folding and chilling twice more.
- Roll out the dough and cut it into 8 rectangles. Arrange
  the chocolate in 2 lines across each rectangle, then roll
  them up and transfer to a lined baking tray.
- Cover the croissants with oiled cling film and leave to rise
  for 1 hour.
- Preheat the oven to 200°C (180°C fan) / 400F / gas 6.
- Brush with egg white and bake for 30 minutes, reducing
  the heat to 180°C (160°C fan) / 350F / gas 4 after 10
  minutes.
- Once cooked, transfer the croissants onto a plate and
  drizzle with the melted chocolate before serving.

Main meals

Mixed vegetable pizza

PREPARATION TIME: 2 hours, 30 minutes
COOKING TIME: 10–12 minutes
MAKES: 2

400 g / 14 oz / 2 ⅔ cups strong white bread flour, plus extra for dusting

½ tsp easy-blend dried yeast

2 tsp caster (superfine) sugar

1 tsp fine sea salt

1 tbsp olive oil

140 ml / 5 fl. oz / ⅔ cup warm water

4 tbsp passata

150 g / 5 oz mozzarella, grated

6 button mushrooms, sliced

½ head broccoli, chopped

1 red pepper, sliced

1 yellow pepper, chopped

2 tsp dried oregano

a handful of rocket (arugula), to garnish

freshly ground black pepper

- Mix together the flour, yeast, sugar and salt and stir the oil into the warm water.

- Stir the liquid into the dry ingredients then knead on a lightly oiled surface for 10 minutes or until smooth and elastic.

- Leave the dough to rest covered with oiled cling film for 1–2 hours until doubled in size.

- Preheat the oven to 220°C (200°C fan) / 425F / gas 7 and grease 2 non-stick baking trays.

- Knead the dough for 2 more minutes then divide in half and roll out into 2 circles.

- Transfer the bases to the baking trays, then spread on the passata and cheese.

- Arrange the vegetables on top and sprinkle with oregano, then bake for 10–12 minutes or until the base is cooked through underneath. Garnish with some rocket leaves and freshly ground black pepper.

Sun-dried tomato and artichoke pizza
Replace the broccoli and peppers with marinated artichokes and sun-dried tomatoes for a succulent Mediterranean pizza.

Béchamel cannelloni

PREPARATION TIME: 40–45 minutes
COOKING TIME: 15 minutes
SERVES: 4

2 tbsp butter
2 tsp olive oil
2 cloves garlic, chopped
1 kg / 2 lb 3 oz spinach leaves
¼ nutmeg, grated
400 g / 14 oz / 1 ¾ cups ricotta
2 tbsp vegetarian Parmesan, grated
12 cannelloni tubes

FOR THE BÉCHAMEL SAUCE
1 white onion, halved
2 cloves
500 ml / 17 ½ fl. oz / 2 cups whole milk
1 bay leaf
50 g / 1 ¾ oz / ¼ cup butter
50 g / 1 ¾ oz / ⅓ cup plain (all-purpose) flour

- Preheat the oven to 180°C (160°C fan) / 350F / gas 4. To make the filling, heat the butter in a pan with the olive oil and cook the garlic for 2 minutes. Add the spinach and nutmeg and stir until wilted.

- Spoon into a sieve and press down firmly with a wooden spoon to extract as much liquid as possible. Once done, finely chop the spinach and leave to cool in a bowl. Then, stir in the ricotta, vegetarian Parmesan and seasoning.

- Spoon into the cannelloni tubes, then lay in a greased baking dish.

- To make the béchamel sauce, stud the halved onion with the cloves and place in a pan with the milk and bay leaf. Bring to the boil and then turn off the heat and leave the milk to infuse for 20 minutes.

- Melt the butter in another pan then add the flour. Stir until a paste forms. Continue to cook for 2 minutes.

- Remove the onion and bay leaf from the milk. Stir the milk into the flour paste until fully incorporated. Cook for 5–10 minutes until the sauce has thickened. Spoon over the cannelloni and bake for around 15 minutes until bubbling. Serve 3 tubes per person and garnish with basil leaves and black pepper.

Tomato cannelloni
For something a little lighter, try this simple tomato sauce: heat 2 tablespoons of olive oil in a pan, then add 1 clove of chopped garlic and two 400 g / 14 oz cans of chopped tomatoes. Leave to simmer, topped up with a little water, for 10 minutes, then add some fresh basil.

Mixed vegetable omelette

PREPARATION TIME: 1 minute
COOKING TIME: 4–5 minutes
SERVES: 1

3 large eggs
1 tbsp butter
a handful of cherry tomatoes
a handful of button mushrooms, sliced
6 baby new potatoes, parboiled and sliced
a handful of spring onions (scallions), chopped
fresh basil leaves, to garnish

- Break the eggs into a jug. Beat them gently to break up the yolks.
- Heat the butter in a non-stick frying pan until sizzling then pour in the eggs. Add the tomatoes, mushrooms potatoes and spring onions, spreading them evenly.
- Cook over a medium heat until the eggs start to set around the outside. Use a spatula to draw the side of the omelette into the middle and tilt the pan to fill the gaps with more liquid egg.
- Repeat the process until the top of the omelette is just set.
- Serve with some fresh basil leaves to garnish. Season to taste and serve while hot.

Mixed vegetable and cheese omelette
Add a handful of grated cheese to the egg mixture, and then a sprinkling over the finished omelette for a light cheesy alternative.

Red pepper lasagne

PREPARATION TIME: **5 minutes**
COOKING TIME: **50 minutes**
SERVES: **4**

2 tbsp olive oil
1 red onion, finely chopped
2 red peppers, diced
2 cloves garlic, crushed
100 g / 3 ½ oz fresh spinach
400 g / 14 oz can tomatoes, chopped
300 g / 10 ½ oz fresh lasagne sheets
2 tbsp vegetarian Parmesan, finely grated

• Heat the oil in a saucepan and fry the onion
  and red pepper for 3 minutes, stirring
  occasionally.
• Add the garlic and cook for 2 minutes, then
  add the spinach and tomatoes.
• Bring the mixture to the boil and simmer for
  10–15 minutes.
• Preheat the oven to 190°C (170°C fan) / 375F /
  gas 5.
• Oil a large baking dish and line it with
  lasagne sheets.
• Add half of the vegetable mixture, then top
  with another layer of lasagne sheets.
• Spoon the rest of the vegetables on top,
  followed by the rest of the lasagne sheets then
  sprinkle with the vegetarian Parmesan.
• Transfer the dish to the oven and bake for
  30 minutes or until cooked through and
  golden brown.

Pepper and black olive lasagne
Add some chopped black olives to the vegetable
mixture for added texture and saltiness.

Arancini

PREPARATION TIME: 15–20 minutes
COOKING TIME: 4–5 minutes
MAKES: 16

4 tbsp plain (all-purpose) flour
1 egg, beaten
75 g / 2 ⅔ oz / 1 cup breadcrumbs
450 g / 1 lb / 2 ¼ cups risotto rice, cooked
100 g / 3 ½ oz mozzarella, grated
sunflower oil, for deep-frying
chopped chives, to serve
tomato sauce, to serve

- Put the flour, egg and breadcrumbs in three separate bowls.
- Mix the rice with the cheese then shape it into 16 balls.
- Dip the arancini alternately in the flour, egg and breadcrumbs and shake off any excess.
- Heat the oil in a deep-fat fryer, according to the manufacturer's instructions, to a temperature of 180°C / 350F.
- Lower the arancini in the fryer basket and cook for 4–5 minutes, until crisp and golden. Tip the arancini into a kitchen-paper-lined bowl to remove any excess oil.
- Garnish and serve with chives and tomato sauce.

Potato and pepper croquettes
To make croquettes, replace the rice with the same amount of mashed potato and add some chopped red peppers. This recipe works well with either mozzarella or Cheddar cheese.

Mediterranean tart

PREPARATION TIME: **40 minutes**
COOKING TIME: **40 minutes**
SERVES: **4**

4 tbsp passata
2 tbsp tomato pesto
1 white onion, sliced
2 beefsteak tomatoes, roughly chopped
1 medium courgette (zucchini), sliced
1 red pepper, chopped
1 yellow pepper, chopped
a small sprig of rosemary

FOR THE PASTRY
100 g / 3 ½ oz / ½ cup butter, cubed
200 g / 7 oz / 1 ⅓ cups plain (all-purpose) flour

- For the pastry, rub the butter into the flour and add just enough cold water to bind.
- Chill for 30 minutes then roll out on a floured surface.
- Preheat the oven to 200°C (180°C fan) / 400F / gas 6.
- Line a medium-sized round baking tray with pastry and prick with a fork. Then line the pastry with oven-safe cling film and fill with baking beans then blind bake for 10 minutes.
- Once the pastry is ready, mix the passata and pesto together and spread evenly across the base of the tart.
- Add the chopped vegetables on top and garnish with the rosemary. Season to taste.
- Bake the tart for 25 minutes or until the pastry is golden brown and cooked through.
- Garnish with salt and pepper and then serve.

Classic ratatouille

PREPARATION TIME: **10 minutes**
COOKING TIME: **40 minutes**
SERVES: **4**

4 tbsp olive oil
2 white onions, peeled and finely sliced
2 aubergines (eggplants), cut in half lengthways and finely sliced
3 courgettes (zucchinis), cut in half lengthways and finely sliced
2 cloves garlic, finely chopped
1 red pepper, seeded and cut into strips
1 green pepper, seeded and cut into strips
1 yellow pepper, seeded and cut into strips
400g / 14 oz can chopped tomatoes
1 tsp dried oregano
a handful of fresh oregano
crusty white bread, to serve

- Heat the oil in a pan and cook the onions until deep golden.
- Add the aubergines and cook for 2 minutes, then add the courgettes and garlic. Cook for 2 minutes, then add the peppers and cook for a further 5 minutes.
- Add the tomatoes and dried oregano and leave to simmer for at least 30 minutes over a very low heat, stirring occasionally, until the vegetables are very soft.
- Season and sprinkle over the fresh oregano before serving with some bread.

Ratatouille with sun-dried tomatoes
Add 75 g / 2 ⅔ oz / ⅓ cup of chopped sun-dried tomatoes to the ratatouille about 10 minutes before the end of the cooking time.

Mashed potatoes with dill

PREPARATION TIME: **5 minutes**
COOKING TIME: **20 minutes**
SERVES: **4**

900 g / 2 lb potatoes, peeled and cubed
150 g / 5 oz / ⅔ cup butter, cubed
2 cloves garlic, minced
1 leek, trimmed and sliced
2 tbsp fresh dill, chopped
250 ml / 9 fl. oz / 1 cup milk

- Cook the potatoes in boiling salted water for 12 minutes or until tender.
- Tip the potatoes into a colander and leave to drain.
- Put the saucepan back on the heat and add the butter. Fry the garlic, leeks and dill in the butter for 5 minutes, then pour in the milk and bring to a simmer.
- Take the pan off the heat and add the potatoes, then mash until smooth. Season to taste with salt and freshly ground black pepper.
- Serve with vegetarian sausages or roasted vegetables.

Vegan mash with dill
For a vegan alternative to this humble classic, swap the butter for the same amount of vegan butter or margarine and replace the milk with a dairy-free alternative.

Haricot and pasta hotpot

PREPARATION TIME: **overnight**
COOKING TIME: **2 hours**
SERVES: **4**

2 tbsp olive oil
1 onion, finely chopped
2 carrots, sliced
a few sprigs of thyme
400 g / 14 oz / 2 ⅔ cups dried haricot beans, soaked overnight
1 litre / 1 pint 15 fl. oz / 4 cups vegetable stock
400 g / 14 oz can tomatoes, chopped
250 g / 9 oz packet gnocchetti (small-cut pasta)
fresh thyme, to garnish
focaccia, to serve

- Heat the oil in a large cast-iron casserole dish and add the onion, carrots and thyme and fry for 5 minutes.
- Drain the beans and add them to the pan with the stock and bring to the boil.
- Turn down the heat and simmer with the lid on for 1 hour 30 minutes or until the beans are tender.
- Drain half of the stock and add the chopped tomatoes and pasta. Simmer for a further 20 minutes, or according to the packet instructions.
- Once the pasta is cooked and the liquid is thick and creamy, divide between 4 serving bowls.
- Garnish with some fresh thyme and season to taste. Serve hot with some fresh focaccia.

Haricot and Parmesan hotpot
Sprinkle some vegetarian Parmesan shavings on top for a deliciously sharp taste.

Penne with tomatoes and vegetarian sausages

PREPARATION TIME: **2 minutes**
COOKING TIME: **30–35 minutes**
SERVES: **4**

4 tbsp olive oil
2 cloves garlic, crushed
1 tsp fennel seeds
4 vegetarian sausages
400 g / 14 oz can tomatoes, chopped
400 g / 14 oz penne pasta
fresh basil, to garnish
vegetarian Parmesan shavings, to garnish

- Heat the oil in a frying pan and fry the garlic and fennel seeds for 2 minutes.
- Add the vegetarian sausages, breaking them up with a spatula as they brown.
- Stir in the canned tomatoes and simmer for 25 minutes.
- Meanwhile, cook the penne in boiling salted water according to the packet instructions, or until al dente.
- Taste the sauce for seasoning, adding plenty of freshly ground black pepper.
- Drain the pasta and stir it into the sauce.
- Garnish with some basil and vegetarian Parmesan before serving.

Vegetable penne with tomatoes
Replace the vegetarian sausages with some mixed vegetables for a wholesome and healthy alternative.

Bean chilli

PREPARATION TIME: 10 minutes
COOKING TIME: 30 minutes
SERVES: 4

2 tbsp olive oil
1 onion, finely chopped
1 red chilli (chili), finely chopped
2 cloves garlic, crushed
400 g / 14 oz / 2 ⅔ cups mushrooms, sliced
1 tsp cayenne pepper
400 g / 14 oz can tomatoes, chopped
200 ml / 6 ¾ fl. oz / ¾ cup vegetable stock
400 g / 14 oz can kidney beans, drained
400 g / 14 oz can cannellini beans, drained
soured cream, to serve
fresh basil leaves, to serve

- Heat the oil in a large saucepan and fry the onion and chilli for 3 minutes, stirring occasionally.
- Add the garlic, mushrooms and cayenne and cook for 2 minutes, then add the chopped tomatoes, stock and beans. Bring to a gentle simmer.
- Cook the chilli for 20 minutes, stirring occasionally, until the sauce has thickened a little.
- Taste for seasoning and add salt and freshly ground black pepper as necessary.
- Serve with soured cream and garnish with some fresh basil leaves.

Bean chilli with guacamole
Serve the chilli with some home-made guacamole. Simply mash the flesh of 2 Hass avocados and add the juice of a lime, a pinch of salt, 1 tablespoon of olive oil and 1 teaspoon of chilli (chili) flakes.

Baked red pepper omelette

PREPARATION TIME: **10 minutes**
COOKING TIME: **30 minutes**
SERVES: **1**

4 eggs
1 tbsp crème fraiche
1 red pepper, deseeded and roughly chopped
1 clove garlic, crushed
1 bunch of parsley, chopped
2 tbsp olive oil
2 tbsp fresh chives, to garnish
rocket (arugula) leaves, washed, to garnish

- Preheat the oven to 200°C (180°C fan) / 400F / gas 6.
- Beat the eggs with the crème fraiche in a large bowl.
- Add the pepper, garlic and parsley, then season and mix together carefully.
- Oil a large frying pan, then pour the mixture in and bake for about 30 minutes until puffed and golden. The egg should be cooked through.
- Fold the omelette and garnish with some slices of red pepper, chives and rocket leaves.
- Season to taste and serve warm or cold.

Red pepper and feta omelette
Replace the crème fraiche with some crumbled feta, reserving some to sprinkle on the omelette once cooked.

Sautéed mushroom tagliatelle

PREPARATION TIME: **5 minutes**
COOKING TIME: **12–15 minutes**
SERVES: **4**

400 g / 14 oz tagliatelle
2 tbsp olive oil
150 g / 5 oz / 1 cup mushrooms, sliced
2 cloves garlic, crushed
2 tbsp flat-leaf parsley, finely chopped

- Boil the pasta in water according to the packet instructions, or until al dente.
- Meanwhile, heat the olive oil in a large sauté pan and sauté the mushrooms for 8 minutes.
- Stir in the garlic and half the parsley and fry for 2 more minutes.
- Drain the pasta and stir it into the pan with the mushrooms.
- Divide the pasta between 4 warm bowls and season.
- Garnish with the remaining parsley and serve.

Parmesan mushroom tagliatelle
For a sharper taste, serve the pasta with some grated vegetarian Parmesan on the side.

Cheesy cauliflower bake

PREPARATION TIME: **20 minutes**
COOKING TIME: **20 minutes**
SERVES: **4–6**

1 head cauliflower
100 g / 3 ½ oz / ½ cup butter
2 tbsp plain (all-purpose) flour
1 tsp mustard powder
500 ml / 17 ½ fl. oz / 2 cups milk
2 bay leaves
grated nutmeg
½ tsp mace
125 g / 4 ⅓ oz / 1 ¼ cups Cheddar cheese, grated
125 g / 4 ⅓ oz / 1 ¼ cups Red Leicester cheese, grated

- Cut the cauliflower into florets and cook in boiling salted water for 5 minutes. Drain well and set aside.
- Preheat the oven to 200°C (180°C fan) / 400F / gas 6.
- Heat the butter in a pan and whisk in the flour and mustard powder to make a paste.
- Gradually whisk in the milk and stir until thick and smooth. Add the bay leaves, nutmeg and mace and leave to simmer gently, stirring occasionally, for 10 minutes.
- Stir in most of the Cheddar and Red Leicester cheese until melted. Tip the cauliflower into a baking dish and spoon over the sauce. Sprinkle with the remaining cheese and bake for 20 minutes.

Broccoli and cauliflower bake
Add some broccoli and peas to pack in more veggies to this cheesy dish.

Lentil and butternut stew

PREPARATION TIME: **5 minutes**
COOKING TIME: **1 hour, 10 minutes**
SERVES: **4**

1 red onion, finely chopped
4 tbsp olive oil
1 carrot, finely chopped
1 red pepper, finely chopped
2 cloves garlic, crushed
400 g / 14 oz can tomatoes, chopped
600 ml / 1 pint 2 fl. oz / 2 ½ cups vegetable stock
400 g / 14 oz / 2 cups brown lentils
1 small butternut squash, cubed
flat-leaf parsley to garnish

- Fry the onion in the oil for 5 minutes then
  add the carrot, pepper and garlic and cook
  for 2 more minutes.
- Stir in the tomatoes, stock, lentils and squash
  then simmer for up to 1 hour, until the lentils
  are tender.
- Taste for seasoning and add salt and black
  pepper as necessary, then garnish with
  parsley.

Lentil and pumpkin stew
Replace the butternut squash with 1 small
pumpkin, skins removed and chopped. Cook
for the same amount of time and garnish with a
dollop of coconut yogurt.

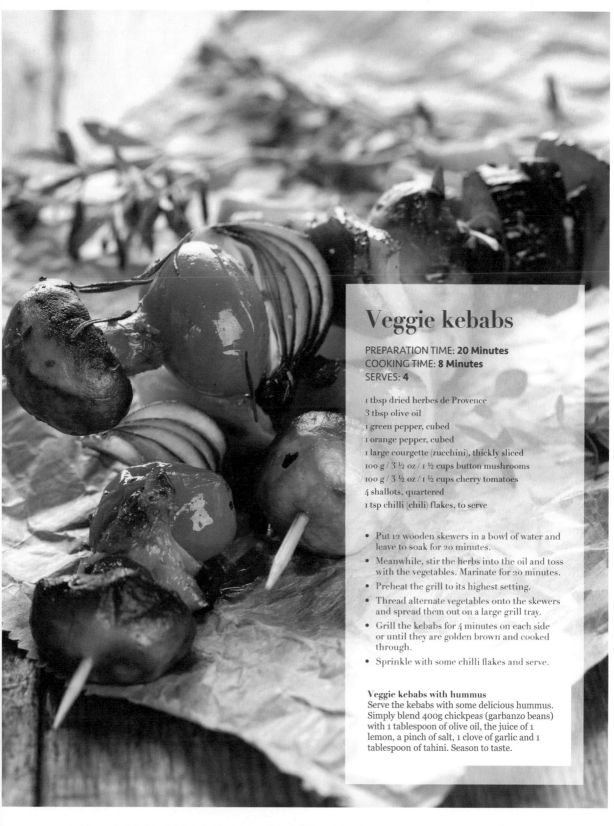

Veggie kebabs

PREPARATION TIME: 20 Minutes
COOKING TIME: 8 Minutes
SERVES: 4

1 tbsp dried herbes de Provence
3 tbsp olive oil
1 green pepper, cubed
1 orange pepper, cubed
1 large courgette (zucchini), thickly sliced
100 g / 3 ½ oz / 1 ½ cups button mushrooms
100 g / 3 ½ oz / 1 ½ cups cherry tomatoes
4 shallots, quartered
1 tsp chilli (chili) flakes, to serve

- Put 12 wooden skewers in a bowl of water and leave to soak for 20 minutes.
- Meanwhile, stir the herbs into the oil and toss with the vegetables. Marinate for 20 minutes.
- Preheat the grill to its highest setting.
- Thread alternate vegetables onto the skewers and spread them out on a large grill tray.
- Grill the kebabs for 4 minutes on each side or until they are golden brown and cooked through.
- Sprinkle with some chilli flakes and serve.

Veggie kebabs with hummus
Serve the kebabs with some delicious hummus. Simply blend 400g chickpeas (garbanzo beans) with 1 tablespoon of olive oil, the juice of 1 lemon, a pinch of salt, 1 clove of garlic and 1 tablespoon of tahini. Season to taste.

Broccoli and cheese pie

PREPARATION TIME: 10 minutes
COOKING TIME: 40–45 minutes
SERVES: 4

2 tbsp olive oil
1 small onion, finely chopped
2 tbsp fresh thyme leaves
2 cloves garlic, crushed
450 g / 1 lb broccoli, (stalks removed) roughly chopped
200 ml / 6 ¾ fl. oz / ¾ cup vegetable stock
450 g / 1 lb potatoes, peeled and cut into cubes
100 ml / 3 ½ fl. oz / ½ cup milk
50 g / 1 ¾ oz / ¼ cup butter
50 g / 1 ¾ oz / ½ cup Cheddar cheese, grated

- Heat the oil in a large saucepan and fry the onion and thyme for 3 minutes, stirring occasionally.
- Add the garlic and cook for 2 minutes, then add the broccoli and pour in the stock. Simmer gently for 10 minutes.
- Taste for seasoning and add salt and freshly ground black pepper as necessary.
- Meanwhile, cook the potatoes in salted water for 15–20 minutes, or until they are tender, then drain well.
- Return the potatoes to the saucepan and add the milk, butter and cheese. Mash the potatoes until smooth.
- Preheat the oven to 200°C (180°C fan) / 400F / gas 6.
- Spoon the broccoli mixture into a baking dish then top with the mashed potatoes.
- Bake the pie for 20 minutes or until golden brown on top.

Mushroom and cheese pie
Replace the broccoli with 450 g / 1 lb mixed mushrooms. Lightly fry the chopped mushrooms in a pan with the garlic, onion and thyme for 10 minutes, before adding the stock.

Poached egg with griddled asparagus

PREPARATION TIME: 25 minutes
COOKING TIME: 8–10 minutes
SERVES: 2

16 asparagus spears
3 tbsp olive oil
2 eggs
½ lemon

- Soak 4 wooden skewers in a bowl of water for 20 minutes.
- Heat a griddle pan until smoking hot.
- Skewer 4 asparagus spears together with each skewer. Brush them liberally with olive oil.
- Sprinkle with plenty of sea salt and black pepper, then cook for 4 minutes on each side on the griddle.
- For the eggs, fill a saucepan with water and bring the water to boil. Crack the eggs one at a time into a small bowl and gently tip into the simmering water. Lightly poach for 3 minutes.
- Divide the asparagus between two plates and remove each egg with a slotted spoon. Cut through the yolk a little, so it pours over the asparagus.
- Squeeze over the lemon, season and serve.

Baked tomatoes with risotto

PREPARATION TIME: 15 minutes
COOKING TIME: 10–12 minutes
SERVES: 2–3

2 tbsp olive oil
2 cloves garlic, minced
1 tsp dried oregano
1 tsp dried basil
6 large vine tomatoes
250 g / 9 oz / 1 ½ cups cooked Arborio rice
a few sprigs of oregano
1 lemon, juiced

- Preheat the oven to 190°C (170°C fan) / 375F / gas 5.
- Heat the oil in a large sauté pan set over a moderate heat.
- Sauté the garlic for 30 seconds and then add the dried herbs and seasoning to taste.
- Remove to one side to cool as you prepare the tomatoes.
- Remove their tops and reserve to one side before scooping out the seeds.
- Fill the tomatoes with the rice and garlic herb mixture, some oregano sprigs and a squeeze of lemon juice and replace the tomato tops.
- Place the stuffed tomatoes on a baking tray and bake for 10–12 minutes until warmed through.
- Remove from the oven and garnish with oregano before serving.

Mozzarella risotto stuffed tomatoes
Divide 50 g / 1 ¾ oz chopped mozzarella between the tomatoes before filling with the cooked rice and baking.

Classic Yorkshire puddings

PREPARATION TIME: **5–10 minutes**
COOKING TIME: **25 minutes**
MAKES: **6**

6 tsp cooking oil
75 g / 2 ⅔ oz / ½ cup plain (all-purpose) flour
2 large eggs
100 ml / 3 ½ fl. oz / ½ cup whole milk
1 pinch nutmeg, grated

- Preheat the oven to 230°C (210°C fan) / 450F / gas 8.
- Put a teaspoon of cooking oil into each hole of a deep 6-hole muffin tin and put it in the oven to heat.
- Put the flour in a large jug with a pinch of salt and make a well in the middle.
- Break in the eggs and pour in the milk then use a whisk to incorporate all the flour from around the outside.
- Add some freshly grated nutmeg and season to taste with salt and pepper.
- Carefully take the muffin tin out of the oven and immediately divide the batter between the holes.
- Return the tin to the oven and bake for 25 minutes without opening the oven door.
- Serve straight away.

Herby cauliflower with cheese
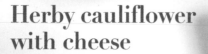

PREPARATION TIME: **10 minutes**
COOKING TIME: **40 minutes**
SERVES: **4**

400 g / 14 oz cauliflower, broken into florets
2 tbsp butter
2 tbsp plain (all-purpose) flour
600 ml / 1 pint 2 fl. oz / 2 ½ cups milk
1 tbsp Dijon mustard
150 g / 5 ½ oz Cheddar cheese, grated
150 g / 5 ½ oz mozzarella cheese, grated
1 tsp mixed dried herbs
nutmeg, grated
fresh flat-leaf parsley, to garnish

- Preheat the oven to 180°C (160°C fan) / 350F / gas 4.
- Cook the cauliflower in boiling, salted water for 6 minutes or until al dente, then drain well.
- Melt the butter in a medium saucepan then stir in the flour.
- Gradually whisk in the milk a little at a time until it is all incorporated.
- Cook the sauce over a low heat, stirring constantly, until the mixture thickens. Beat vigorously to remove any lumps.
- Take the pan off the heat and stir in the cauliflower, mustard, dried herbs and half of the cheese. Season to taste with salt and pepper.
- Spoon the mixture into a baking dish and sprinkle over the rest of the cheese. Add some grated nutmeg on top before baking.
- Bake for 25 minutes or until the top is golden brown. Sprinkle some fresh parsley on top before serving.

Spinach and ricotta lasagne

PREPARATION TIME: **5 minutes**
COOKING TIME: **45 minutes**
SERVES: **4**

2 tbsp olive oil
1 red onion, finely chopped
1 red pepper, diced
2 cloves garlic, crushed
100 g / 3 ½ oz spinach
400 g / 14 oz can tomatoes, chopped
300 g / 10 ½ oz fresh lasagne sheets
200 g / 7 oz ricotta cheese
2 tbsp vegetarian Parmesan, finely grated

- Heat the oil in a large saucepan and fry the onion and red pepper for 3 minutes, stirring occasionally.
- Add the garlic and cook for 2 minutes, then add the spinach and tomatoes.
- Bring the mixture to the boil and simmer for 10 minutes.
- Preheat the oven to 190°C (170°C fan) / 375F / gas 5.
- Oil a large baking dish and line it with lasagne sheets.
- Add half of the spinach mixture, then top with some ricotta and another layer of pasta.
- Spoon some more of the spinach mixture on top, followed by some more ricotta and the rest of the lasagne then repeat this step and sprinkle with Parmesan.
- Transfer the dish to the oven and bake for 30 minutes or until cooked through and golden brown.

Spinach and mozzarella lasagne
Swap the ricotta for 200 g / 7 oz smoked or plain mozzarella and follow the same method above.

Veggie sausages and mash

PREPARATION TIME: 2 Minutes
COOKING TIME: 15 Minutes
SERVES: 4

900 g / 2 lb / 6 cup potatoes, peeled and cubed
250 ml / 9 fl. oz / 1 cup whole milk
150 g / 5 ½ oz / ½ cup butter, cubed
8 cooked vegetarian sausages, to serve
gravy, to serve
fresh oregano, to serve

- Put the potatoes in a pan of cold, salted water and bring to the boil.
- Cook the potatoes for 10 minutes or until tender all the way through.
- Tip the potatoes into a colander and leave to drain.
- Put the saucepan back on the heat and add the milk and butter. Heat until the milk starts to simmer, then return the potatoes to the pan.
- Take the pan off the heat and mash with a potato masher until smooth. Season to taste with salt and pepper and serve.
- Serve with the cooked vegetarian sausages and pour over some gravy. Sprinkle with the fresh oregano.

Vegan sausages and mash
For a vegan version, replace the whole milk with dairy-free milk and the butter with vegan butter or margarine. Make sure the sausages are vegan and don't contain egg.

Two-cheese lasagne

PREPARATION TIME: 5 Minutes
COOKING TIME: 20 Minutes
SERVES: 4

2 tbsp olive oil
1 red onion, finely chopped
200 g / 7 oz cherry tomatoes, chopped
2 cloves of garlic, crushed
100 g / 3 ½ oz fresh spinach
400 g / 14 oz / 2 ⅔ cups canned tomatoes, chopped
300 g / 10 ½ oz fresh lasagne sheets
100 g / 3 ½ oz / ½ cup mozzarella, grated
a handful of vegetarian Parmesan shavings
fresh basil leaves, to serve

- Heat the oil in a large saucepan and fry the onion and tomatoes for 3 minutes, stirring occasionally.
- Add the garlic and cook for 2 minutes, then add the spinach and tomatoes.
- Bring the mixture to the boil and simmer for 10 minutes.
- Preheat the oven to 190°C (170°C fan) / 375F / gas 5.
- Oil a large baking dish and line it with lasagne sheets.
- Add half of the vegetable mixture, then top with another layer of pasta and half of the mozzarella.
- Spoon the rest of the vegetables on top, followed by the rest of the lasagne then sprinkle with Parmesan and the rest of the mozzarella.
- Transfer the dish to the oven and bake for 30 minutes or until cooked through and golden brown.
- Garnish with some fresh basil leaves before serving.

Cheesy vegan lasagne
Replace the mozzarella with 100 g / 3 ½ oz / ½ cup vegan mozzarella, grated. Swap the Parmesan for a vegan version.

Penne with basil pesto

PREPARATION TIME: **10 minutes**
COOKING TIME: **15–20 minutes**
SERVES: **4**

1 tbsp olive oil
150 g / 5 oz / 1 cup peas, fresh or defrosted
400 g / 14 oz penne pasta

FOR THE PESTO
1 tbsp extra-virgin olive oil
a handful of cashew nuts
1 tbsp pine nuts
½ garlic clove
½ lemon, juiced
a handful of fresh basil leaves, plus extra
for garnish

- To make the pesto, simply add all the pesto
  ingredients to a blender and pulse to the
  desired texture and creaminess. Add a little
  water as you go.
- Heat the pasta in salted boiling water for
  15 minutes or until al dente, as per the
  packet's instructions.
- Then, heat a saucepan with the oil and add
  the peas and tomatoes and cook for about
  3–4 minutes.
- Once the pasta is ready and the peas are
  tender, stir in the pesto until the pasta is
  evenly coated.
- Divide between 4 warm bowls and serve
  immediately, garnished with fresh basil.

Penne with sun-dried tomatoes
Add some chopped sun-dried tomatoes instead
of the cherry tomatoes. Alternatively, add the
sun-dried tomatoes to the pesto ingredients
before blending.

Mint couscous salad

PREPARATION TIME: 15 minutes
SERVES: 2

300 g / 10 ½ oz / 1 ¾ cups couscous
8 cherry tomatoes, chopped into small wedges
5 mint leaves, washed
1 stick celery, chopped into small pieces
a handful of flat-leaf parsley, chopped into thin pieces
drizzle of olive oil

- Place the couscous in a large bowl and pour over enough boiling water to just cover the top of the couscous. Leave it to swell for 6–8 minutes, or until fluffy and soft.
- Meanwhile, in a separate bowl, mix together the cherry tomato wedges, mint leaves, celery and chopped parsley with the olive oil.
- Add the fluffy couscous to the bowl and stir well to combine. Drizzle over more olive oil as desired.
- Divide into 2 smaller bowls and serve.

Two-pepper paella

PREPARATION TIME: 5 minutes
COOKING TIME: 30 minutes
SERVES: 4

1 litre / 1 pint 15 fl. oz / 4 cups vegetable stock
4 tbsp olive oil
1 onion, finely chopped
2 cloves garlic, crushed
1 red pepper, sliced
1 yellow pepper, sliced
200 g / 7 oz / 1 ⅓ cups peas, fresh or frozen
200 g / 7 oz / 1 cup paella rice
1 tsp saffron (optional)

- Heat the stock in a saucepan.
- Heat the olive oil in a paella pan and gently fry the onion for 5 minutes without browning.
- Add the garlic and cook for 2 more minutes, then stir in the red pepper, yellow pepper, peas and rice and a little seasoning.
- Stir well to coat with the oil, then pour in the stock and stir once more.
- Bring to a simmer, then cook without stirring for 10 minutes.
- Cover the pan with foil or a lid, turn off the heat and leave to stand for 10 minutes. Uncover the pan and sprinkle over the saffron before serving.

Courgette and asparagus paella
For extra veggies, cut 100 g / 3 ½ oz asparagus spears into short lengths and add to the paella with 1 sliced courgette (zucchini).

Roasted Mediterranean vegetables

PREPARATION TIME: **5 minutes**
COOKING TIME: **25–30 minutes**
SERVES: **4**

4 cloves garlic, chopped
1 white onion, chopped
2 courgettes (zucchinis), sliced
1 red pepper, chopped
1 large aubergine (eggplant), chopped
3 tbsp olive oil
½ lemon, juiced
fresh basil leaves

- Preheat the oven to 200°C (180°C fan) / 400F / gas 6.
- Toss all the vegetables together in a large baking tray with the oil and season well.
- Place the baking tray in the oven for 25–30 minutes or until the vegetables are cooked through and starting to brown.
- Once cooked, remove from the oven and add a squeeze of lemon juice. Season to taste and sprinkle some basil leaves over the top.
- Serve hot or cold.

Parmesan penne with basil

PREPARATION TIME: 5 minutes
COOKING TIME: 12–15 minutes
SERVES: 4

400 g / 14 oz rainbow penne pasta
3 tbsp basil leaves, finely chopped
50 g / 1 ¾ oz / ½ cup vegetarian Parmesan, finely grated
a few sprigs of basil, to serve

- Cook the penne in boiling salted water according to the packet instructions, or until al dente.
- Drain the pasta, reserving a few tablespoons of the cooking water, then return it to the pan and toss with the basil and Parmesan.
- If the pasta begins to look dry, add a little of the pasta water to thin it.
- Divide between 4 warm bowls and serve immediately, garnished with basil sprigs.

Classic tomato and basil penne
Use normal penne and simmer 400 g / 14 oz of canned tomatoes with 2 cloves of crushed garlic and 2 tablespoons of olive oil. Season to taste with salt and pepper.

Rainbow stir-fry

PREPARATION TIME: **15 minutes**
COOKING TIME: **6 minutes**
SERVES: **4**

2 tbsp vegetable oil
2 cloves garlic, finely chopped
3 shallots, sliced
1 tbsp root ginger, finely chopped
2 stalks celery, chopped
1 courgette (zucchini), sliced
1 red pepper, roughly chopped
2 tomatoes, cut into wedges
2 medium-sized carrots, finely sliced
2 tbsp rice wine or dry sherry
1 tsp caster (superfine) sugar
1 tbsp light soy sauce
1 sprig rosemary, chopped

- Heat the oil in a large wok and fry the garlic, shallots and ginger for 30 seconds.
- Add the vegetables and stir-fry for 4 minutes.
- Mix the rice wine, sugar and soy together and add it to the wok.
- Stir-fry until the vegetables are cooked through and evenly coated with the sauce. Add the rosemary and season to taste. Serve immediately.

Rainbow tofu stir-fry
Add some smoked tofu and pumpkin seeds for added nutrition. Simple drain any excess liquid from the tofu and cut into cubes, cook with the vegetables. Sprinkle over the seeds before serving.

Green bean and tomato frittata

PREPARATION TIME: 30 minutes
COOKING TIME: 35 minutes
SERVES: 6

8 eggs
1 tbsp crème fraiche
1 packet green beans
1 onion, peeled and thickly sliced
2 tbsp olive oil
18 cherry tomatoes, halved
1 tsp mixed dried herbs
fresh parsley leaves, to garnish

- Preheat the oven to 180°C (160°C fan) / 350F / gas 4.
- Beat the eggs with the crème fraiche in a large bowl.
- Remove the stalks from the green beans and discard. Cut the beans into short lengths.
- Fry the onion gently in 2 tablespoons of olive oil until soft, about 20 minutes.
- Pour the egg mixture in, add the beans and tomatoes and distribute evenly.
- Season with salt and pepper.
- Bake for about 35 minutes until puffed and golden. The egg should be cooked through. Garnish with some mixed dried herbs and fresh parsley leaves.
- Cut into squares and serve warm or cold.

Asparagus and tomato frittata
Replace the green beans with asparagus. Remove the ends and cut into short lengths. Follow the same method for a delicious alternative.

Soba noodle bowl

PREPARATION TIME: **10 minutes**
COOKING TIME: **10 minutes**
SERVES: **4**

250 g / 9 oz soba noodles
2 tbsp sesame oil
2 cloves garlic, finely chopped
3 shallots, sliced
1 tbsp root ginger, finely chopped
2 medium-sized carrots, sliced
200 g / 7 oz / 1 ⅓ cups mangetout
2 tbsp rice wine or dry sherry
2 tbsp light soy sauce
1 sheet nori seaweed, cut into small pieces
fresh chives, chopped

- In a medium-sized pan, bring the water to the boil and add the noodles. Cook for 10 minutes or until al dente, according to the packet instructions.
- Meanwhile, heat the oil in a large wok and fry the garlic, shallots and ginger for 30 seconds.
- Add the vegetables and stir-fry for 4 minutes.
- Mix the rice wine and soy together and add it to the wok.
- Stir-fry until the vegetables are cooked through and evenly coated with the sauce.
- Once the noodles are almost cooked through, add them to the wok and mix together with the vegetables. Add the seaweed and chives and season to taste. Serve immediately.

Twice-cooked potatoes with rosemary salt

PREPARATION TIME: **5 minutes**
COOKING TIME: **55 minutes**
SERVES: **4**

800 g / 1 lb 12 oz new potatoes, halved if large
6 tbsp olive oil
1 garlic bulb, cloves removed, skins on
Szechuan pepper and rosemary salt
2 garlic cloves, crushed
sprig rosemary, roughly chopped
½ lemon, juiced

- Preheat the oven to 200°C (180°C fan) / 400F / gas 6.
- Boil the potatoes in salted water for 10 minutes then drain well and leave to steam dry for 2 minutes.
- Put 4 tablespoons of oil in a roasting tin. Put the roasting tin in the oven to heat for 2 minutes.
- Add the potatoes to the roasting tin. Stir to coat in the oil and add the garlic cloves.
- Roast the potatoes for 30 minutes or until golden brown then sprinkle with Szechuan pepper and rosemary salt.
- Add the semi-roasted potatoes and crushed garlic to a frying pan with the remaining oil, fresh rosemary and lemon juice. Season to taste.
- Fry for a further 10 minutes, then serve.

Smoky twice-cooked potatoes
Replace the rosemary salt with half a teaspoon of smoked salt and half a teaspoon of smoked garlic for a delicious earthy taste.

Miso-glazed aubergine with coconut yogurt

PREPARATION TIME: 5 minutes
COOKING TIME: 30–35 minutes
SERVES: 2

1 large aubergine (eggplant), cut in half lengthways
1 tbsp brown miso paste
1 tbsp maple syrup
½ lemon, juiced
coconut yogurt, to serve
a handful of chopped walnuts, to serve

- Preheat the oven to 200°C (180°C fan) / 400F / gas 6.
- Score the aubergine flesh in a zigzag pattern along the length of the aubergine. Place the aubergine halves on a baking tray flesh-side down and place in the oven for 20 minutes.
- To make the miso glaze, simply combine the miso paste, maple syrup and lemon juice with 1 teaspoon of hot water. Mix well until the consistency is thick and a little runny.
- Remove the aubergine halves from the oven and turn over. The skins should be slightly charred and crispy. Drizzle the miso glaze over the flesh of each and then place back in the oven for 10–15 minutes.
- Once the aubergines are cooked, place on a serving plate and add a dollop of coconut yogurt on top of each. Sprinkle over some chopped walnuts and serve hot.

Chickpea, squash and wild rice soup

PREPARATION TIME: 10 minutes
COOKING TIME: 20–25 minutes
SERVES: 4

2 tbsp olive oil

4 spring onions (scallions), chopped

2 cloves garlic, crushed

1 red pepper, sliced

1 small cooked kaboucha squash, skins removed and chopped

150 g / 5 oz / 1 cup canned chickpeas (garbanzo beans), water drained

250 g / 9 oz / 1 ½ cups cooked wild rice

400 g / 14 oz can tomatoes, chopped

1 litre / 1 pint 15 fl. oz / 4 cups vegetable stock

fresh chives, to serve

- Heat the oil in a saucepan and fry the onions and garlic for 5 minutes or until softened.
- Add the pepper, squash, chickpeas and wild rice to the pan and cook for 2 more minutes, then stir in the chopped tomatoes and vegetable stock and bring to the boil.
- Simmer for 10–15 minutes then season to taste with salt and pepper.
- Ladle the soup into 4 warm bowls and garnish with parsley.

Chickpea, sweet potato and wild rice soup
Replace the squash with diced sweet potato for an equally delicious and hearty soup.

Rustic pizza margarita

PREPARATION TIME: 2 hours, 30 minutes
COOKING TIME: 10–12 minutes
MAKES: 1

200 g / 7 oz / 1 ⅓ cups whole wheat bread flour, plus extra for dusting
½ tsp easy-blend dried yeast
1 tsp caster (superfine) sugar
½ tsp fine sea salt
1 tbsp olive oil, plus extra for drizzling
140 ml / 5 fl. oz / ⅔ cup warm water
3 tbsp passata
150 g / 5 oz mozzarella, sliced
4 large slices beefsteak tomato
fresh basil leaves

- Mix together the flour, yeast, sugar and salt and stir the oil into the warm water.
- Stir the liquid into the dry ingredients then knead on a lightly oiled surface for 10 minutes or until smooth and elastic.
- Leave the dough to rest covered with oiled cling film for 1–2 hours until doubled in size.
- Preheat the oven to 220°C (200°C fan) / 425F / gas 7 and grease a non-stick baking tray.
- Knead the dough for 2 more minutes then roll out thinly into a circle with thick edges and transfer to the baking tray.
- Spread the dough with the passata and top with the mozzarella, followed by the tomato and basil. Drizzle with olive oil and sprinkle with salt and pepper.
- Transfer the tray to the oven and bake for 10–12 minutes or until the pizza dough is cooked through underneath.

Pizza marinara
Add 1 crushed clove of garlic to the pizza base and swap the basil for oregano. Omit the mozzarella and you have your pizza.

Smoked paprika potato wedges

PREPARATION TIME: **5 minutes**
COOKING TIME: **35–40 minutes**
SERVES: **4**

4 tbsp olive oil
800 g / 1 lb 12 oz potatoes, cut into wedges
1 tsp smoked paprika
parsley leaves, to garnish
tomato sauce, to serve
soured cream, to serve

- Preheat the oven to 220°C (200°C fan) / 425F / gas 7.
- Put the oil in a large roasting tin and heat in the oven for 5 minutes.
- Carefully tip the potato wedges into the pan and turn to coat in the oil and smoked paprika. Season well with salt and black pepper.
- Bake the wedges for 35–40 minutes, turning them every 15 minutes, until golden brown on the outside and fluffy within.
- Sprinkle with a little more sea salt and paprika then garnish with the parsley. Serve with tomato sauce and soured cream.

Smoked paprika sweet potato wedges
Replace the normal potatoes with the same amount of sweet potatoes and follow the method as above. Squeeze the juice of half a lemon on the wedges before serving.

Bean burgers with salad

PREPARATION TIME: 5 minutes
COOKING TIME: 10 minutes
SERVES: 2

2 tbsp olive oil
2 bean burgers
2 tbsp mayonnaise
2 seeded burger buns
½ beefsteak tomato, sliced
½ red onion, sliced finely
a handful of spinach leaves

- Bring a frying pan to medium heat and add the oil.
- Cook the bean burgers for 5 minutes on each side or until cooked through and starting to brown.
- Spread a thick layer of mayonnaise on the flat side of the bottom burger bun. Add a slice of tomato and then layer with the cooked burger, onion slices and some spinach.
- Serve with a side of sweet potato fries or coleslaw for a deliciously simple meal.

Penne with olives and tomato

PREPARATION TIME: 2 minutes
COOKING TIME: 25 minutes
SERVES: 4

4 tbsp olive oil
2 cloves garlic, crushed
400 g / 14 oz can tomatoes, chopped
a handful of pitted olives
400 g / 14 oz penne pasta
1 tbsp vegetarian Parmesan, to serve
fresh basil leaves, to serve

- Heat the oil in a frying pan and fry the garlic for 2 minutes.
- Stir in the canned tomatoes and olives and simmer for 20 minutes.
- Meanwhile, cook the penne in boiling salted water according to the packet instructions or until al dente.
- Taste the sauce for seasoning, adding plenty of freshly ground black pepper.
- Drain the pasta and stir it into the sauce before serving sprinkled with the vegetarian Parmesan and garnish with fresh basil.

Penne puttanesca
Swap the Parmesan for 2 tablespoons of capers and 4 fillets of chopped anchovies.

Cheesy potato bake

PREPARATION TIME: 15 minutes
COOKING TIME: 1 hour, 30 minutes
SERVES: 4

450 g / 1 lb Maris Piper potatoes, thinly sliced
1 clove garlic, halved
50 g / 1 ¾ oz / ¼ cup butter, softened
800 ml / 1 pint 8 fl. oz / 3 ⅓ cups double
(heavy) cream
150 g / 5 oz / 1 ½ cups Cheddar cheese, grated
freshly grated nutmeg, for sprinkling
a handful of fresh cress, to garnish

- Preheat the oven to 180°C (160°C fan) / 350F / gas 4.
- Blanch the potatoes in boiling salted water for 5 minutes then drain well and dry off with a clean tea towel.
- Rub the inside of a baking dish with the halved garlic clove then smear the inside thickly with half of the butter.
- Pour the cream into a big mixing bowl and season well with salt and pepper. Tip in the potatoes and stir well to coat, then tip the lot into the baking dish and level the top.
- Add the grated cheese evenly on top and sprinkle with some nutmeg.
- Dot over the rest of the butter then bake for 1 hour 30 minutes or until the potatoes are completely tender when you insert a skewer in the middle.
- Garnish with some fresh cress. Serve hot.

Two-cheese potato bake
Add 150 g / 5 oz / 1 ½ cups grated Red Leicester cheese to the topping before baking. Mix the grated Cheddar and Red Leicester together before sprinkling on top.

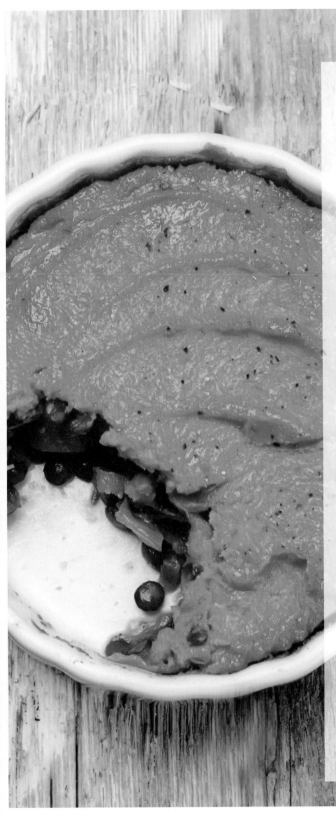

Vegan sweet potato lentil pie

PREPARATION TIME: **2 minutes**
COOKING TIME: **1 hour, 30 minutes**
SERVES: **4**

2 tbsp olive oil
1 small onion, finely chopped
2 cloves of garlic, crushed
1 large red pepper, diced
200 g / 7 oz / 1 2/3 cups chestnut mushrooms, sliced
450 g / 1 lb / 2 cups cooked lentils
400 g / 14 oz / 1 ½ cups canned tomatoes, chopped
400 ml / 14 fl. oz / 1 2/3 cups vegetable stock
freshly ground black pepper

FOR THE TOPPING
2 large sweet potatoes
50 g / 1 ½ oz / ½ cup dairy-free butter
2 tsp fresh thyme leaves

- Preheat the oven to 200°C (180°C fan) / 400F / gas 6.
- Bake the sweet potatoes in their skins for 45 or until a skewer inserted slides in easily.
- Meanwhile, heat the oil in a large saucepan and fry the onion for 3 minutes, stirring occasionally.
- Add the garlic, pepper and mushrooms and cook for 2 minutes, then add the lentils.
- Fry the lentils then add the chopped tomatoes and stock and bring to a gentle simmer.
- Cook for 1 hour, stirring occasionally, until the lentils are tender and the sauce has thickened.
- When the sweet potatoes are ready, peel off and discard the skins and mash the flesh with the butter and thyme leaves.
- Spoon the lentil mixture into a large baking dish then top with the mashed sweet potatoes.
- Use a fork to level the surface and make stripes in the potato then bake in the oven for 20 minutes or until golden brown.
- Sprinkle some black pepper on top before serving.

Goat's cheese potato pie
For a non-vegan version, add some crumbled goat's cheese to the lentil mixture before baking in the oven.

Garlic-stuffed portobello mushrooms

PREPARATION TIME: **1 minute**
COOKING TIME: **20 minutes**
SERVES: **2**

4 large portobello mushrooms
2 tbsp olive oil
4 cloves garlic, chopped
200 g / 7 oz / 2 cups Cheddar cheese, grated
2 tbsp flat-leaf parsley, chopped
1 red chilli (chili), sliced (optional)

- Preheat the oven to 200°C (180°C fan) / 400F / gas 6.
- Remove the stalks from the mushrooms and arrange cut side up in a baking dish.
- Brush the mushrooms with oil and roast for 15 minutes.
- Heat the oil in a frying pan and cook the garlic until it just starts to turn golden, then spoon the garlic over the mushrooms and sprinkle the cheese on top. Top with sliced chillis if desired.
- Bake for a further 5 minutes and then sprinkle with the parsley. Season to taste before serving.

Pesto portobello mushrooms
Omit the Cheddar cheese and replace with pesto mixed with mashed avocado for a delicious creamy alternative. Cook in the oven for 5 minutes before serving.

Ravioli with parsley pesto

PREPARATION TIME: **10 minutes**
COOKING TIME: **5 minutes**
SERVES: **4**

450 g / 1 lb fresh ravioli
1 bunch of flat-leaf parsley, stalks removed
1 clove garlic, crushed
1 lemon, zest finely grated
4 tbsp olive oil
100 g / 3 ½ oz ricotta salata, crumbled
vegetarian Parmesan, to serve

- Cook the ravioli in boiling water according to the packet instructions.
- Meanwhile, wash the parsley leaves, drain well then squeeze out all the liquid.
- Put them in a blender with the garlic, lemon zest and oil and add a pinch of salt and pepper, then blend to a smooth sauce.
- Drain the ravioli and split between 4 bowls.
- Mix the ricotta with the parsley pesto. Serve a generous amount on top of the ravioli.
- Serve with a sprinkling of grated vegetarian Parmesan.

Ravioli with basil pesto
Replace the parsley with basil leaves and serve with some toasted pine nuts on top.

Red onion, rocket and Parmesan pizza

PREPARATION TIME: **2 hours, 30 minutes**
COOKING TIME: **10–12 minutes**
MAKES: **2**

400 g / 14 oz / 2 ⅔ cups strong white bread flour, plus extra for dusting
½ tsp easy-blend dried yeast
2 tsp caster (superfine) sugar
1 tsp fine sea salt
1 tbsp olive oil
140 ml / 5 fl. oz / ⅔ cup warm water
1 red onion, sliced
a handful of green pitted olives, sliced
a handful of rocket (arugula) leaves
150 g / 5 oz / 1 ½ cups vegetarian Parmesan, grated
2 tsp dried oregano

- Mix together the flour, yeast, sugar and salt and stir the oil into the warm water.
- Stir the liquid into the dry ingredients then knead on a lightly oiled surface for 10 minutes or until smooth and elastic.
- Leave the dough to rest covered with oiled cling film for 1–2 hours until doubled in size.
- Preheat the oven to 220°C (200°C fan) / 425F/ gas 7 and grease 2 non-stick baking trays.
- Knead the dough for 2 more minutes then divide in half and roll out into 2 circles.
- Transfer the bases to the baking trays and arrange the red onion, olives, rocket and vegetarian Parmesan on top. Sprinkle with oregano then bake for 10–12 minutes or until the base is cooked through underneath.

Spinach, tomato and artichoke pizza
Replace the rocket and onion with a handful of baby spinach leaves and add some sun-dried tomatoes and artichokes for a delicious alternative.

Bean and carrot hotpot

PREPARATION TIME: **Overnight**
COOKING TIME: **2 hours, 10 minutes**
SERVES: **8**

2 tbsp olive oil
1 onion, finely chopped
2 carrots, sliced
a few sprigs of thyme
400 g / 14 oz / 2 ⅔ cups dried mixed beans, soaked overnight
1 litre / 1 pint 15 fl. oz / 4 cups vegetable stock
flat-leaf parsley, to garnish

- Heat the oil in a large cast-iron casserole dish and add the onion, carrots and thyme and fry for 5 minutes.
- Drain the beans and add them to the pan with the stock and bring to the boil.
- Turn down the heat and simmer with the lid on for 2 hours or until the beans are tender.
- Season to taste, then garnish with parsley then serve immediately.

Bean and Parmesan hotpot
Once served, add some grated vegetarian Parmesan on top.

Aubergine-stuffed portobello mushrooms

PREPARATION TIME: **10 minutes**
COOKING TIME: **35 minutes**
SERVES: **4**

2 beefsteak tomatoes
150 g / 5 oz / ¾ cup sun-dried tomatoes in oil, drained and chopped
150 g / 5 oz aubergine (eggplant) in oil, drained and chopped
8 portobello mushrooms
fresh oregano leaves
fresh parsley leaves, chopped

- Preheat the oven to 200°C (180°C fan) / 400F / gas 6.
- Scoop out the middles of the tomatoes with a teaspoon and chop the flesh into small cubes.
- Combine the sun-dried tomatoes, aubergine and cubed tomato and pack the mixture into the mushroom cavities. Sprinkle the oregano on top and season to taste.
- Bake the mushrooms for 35 minutes or until they are tender all the way through.
- Serve with some fresh parsley leaves on the side.

Cauliflower cheese

PREPARATION TIME: 10 minutes
COOKING TIME: 30 minutes
MAKES: 4

400 g / 14 oz cauliflower, roughly chopped
2 tbsp olive oil
2 tbsp butter
2 tbsp plain (all-purpose) flour
600 ml / 1 pint / 2 ½ cups milk
150 g / 5 ½ oz Cheddar cheese, grated
freshly grated nutmeg for sprinkling
salt freshly ground black pepper
flat-leaf parsley, to garnish

- Preheat the oven to 180°C (160°C fan) / 350F/ gas 4.
- Place the cauliflower on a baking tray with a little oil, salt and pepper. Transfer the tray to the oven and roast the cauliflower for 20 minutes or until slightly brown on top.
- Melt the butter in a saucepan then stir in the flour.
- Gradually whisk in the milk a little at a time until it is all incorporated.
- Cook the sauce over a low heat, stirring, until the mixture thickens. Beat vigorously to remove any lumps.
- Take the pan off the heat and season to taste with salt and pepper.
- Once the cauliflower is cooked, divide between 4 gratin dishes and add the sauce on top. Sprinkle with the remaining cheese.
- Sprinkle with nutmeg and bake for 10 minutes or until the cheese has melted. Garnish with some fresh flat-leaved parsley.

Cauliflower cheese with Red Leicester
Replace the Cheddar cheese with the same amount of Red Leicester cheese for a slightly different flavour.

Ravioli with tomato and basil

PREPARATION TIME: **5 minutes**
COOKING TIME: **5–8 minutes**
SERVES: **4**

450 g / 1 lb fresh ravioli
4 tbsp olive oil
1 white onion, diced
1 clove garlic, crushed
½ lemon, juiced
a handful of black olives, chopped
400 g / 14 oz can tomatoes, chopped
fresh basil leaves, to garnish

- Cook the ravioli in boiling salted water according to the packet instructions or until al dente.
- Heat a saucepan with a little oil. Add the onion, garlic, lemon juice, olives and tomatoes and add a good pinch of salt and pepper. Simmer for 5 minutes.
- Drain the ravioli and split between 4 warm bowls. Spoon over the tomato sauce and top with the basil leaves.

Spaghetti al pomodoro
Replace the ravioli with spaghetti for a classic Italian alternative.

Scrambled egg on toast

PREPARATION TIME: 5 minutes
COOKING TIME: 5 minutes
SERVES: 4

8 large eggs
2 tbsp butter
4 slices wholemeal bread, toasted
a handful of cherry tomatoes, chopped
a handful of fresh chopped chives, to garnish
fresh parsley leaves, to garnish

- Gently beat the eggs to break up the yolks, and season.
- Heat the butter in a non-stick frying pan until sizzling then pour in the eggs.
- Cook over a low heat, stirring constantly until the eggs start to scramble.
- Spoon onto the toasted bread and top with the tomatoes, chives and parsley.

Scrambled tofu on toast
Replace the eggs with tofu. Crumble 1 block of tofu into a frying pan and cook over a low heat. Add half a teaspoon of ground turmeric and season to taste.

Stuffed tomatoes with aubergine

PREPARATION TIME: 10 minutes
COOKING TIME: 35 minutes
SERVES: 4

8 beefsteak tomatoes, halved
a handful of mozzarella, grated
150 g / 5 oz / ¾ cup sun-dried tomatoes in oil, drained and chopped
150 g / 5 oz aubergine (eggplant) in oil, drained and chopped
1 tsp dried basil
fresh basil leaves, to serve

- Preheat the oven to 200°C (180°C fan) / 400F / gas 6.
- Scoop out the middles of the tomatoes with a teaspoon and arrange on a baking tray.
- Mix the mozzarella with the sun-dried tomatoes and aubergine and pack the mixture into the tomato cavities. Sprinkle the dried basil on top.
- Bake the tomatoes for 35 minutes or until they are tender all the way through.
- Serve with some fresh basil leaves on the side.

Aubergine-stuffed onions
Replace the tomatoes with onions. Simply boil 2 large white onions for 10 minutes or until soft. Cut in half and scoop out the insides, then stuff with the aubergine (eggplant) mixture and bake as above.

Chilli and guacamole quesadilla

PREPARATION TIME: **10 minutes**
COOKING TIME: **10–12 minutes**
SERVES: **4**

2 tbsp sunflower oil
1 onion, finely sliced
1 red chilli (chili), sliced
1 red pepper, sliced
2 tbsp fajita seasoning
8 soft flour tortillas
50 g / 1 ¾ oz / ½ cup Cheddar cheese, grated
guacamole, to serve
a sprig of coriander (cilantro), to garnish

- Heat the oil in a large frying pan and stir-fry onions, chilli and peppers with the fajita seasoning for 4 minutes. Set to one side.
- Add a tortilla to the empty pan and warm through until golden brown. Add a handful of grated cheese and a quarter of the onion and pepper mixture and spread evenly.
- Place a second tortilla on top, flatten and flip the tortillas to lightly brown the bottom of the quesadilla.
- Remove the quesadilla from the pan and top with some guacamole. Repeat for all 4 quesadilla.
- Garnish with a little grated cheese and the coriander. Serve immediately.

Chilli rice bowl
Instead of the flour tortilla, serve the pepper mixture with cooked short-grain brown rice.

Butter bean and Parmesan stew

PREPARATION TIME: **Overnight**
COOKING TIME: **2 hours, 15 minutes**
SERVES: **8**

2 tbsp olive oil
1 onion, finely chopped
1 red pepper, sliced
a few sprigs of thyme
400 g / 14 oz / 2 ⅔ cups dried mixed beans (butter beans and chickpeas), soaked overnight
1 litre / 1 pint 15 fl. oz / 4 cups vegetable stock
a handful of spinach leaves
vegetarian Parmesan, to garnish

- Heat the oil in a large cast-iron casserole dish and add the onion, pepper and thyme and fry for 5 minutes.
- Drain the beans and add them to the pan with the stock and bring to the boil.
- Turn down the heat and simmer with the lid on for 2 hours or until the beans are tender.
- Add the spinach leaves and stir well to incorporate.
- Season to taste, then garnish with some Parmesan cheese. Serve hot.

Rosemary potato frittata

PREPARATION TIME: **10 minutes**
COOKING TIME: **35 minutes**
SERVES: **6**

8 eggs
1 tbsp crème fraiche
400 g / 14 oz cooked new potatoes, cubed
1 clove garlic, crushed
1 sprig rosemary, chopped
1 tbsp olive oil

- Preheat the oven to 200°C (180°C fan) / 400F / gas 6.
- Beat the eggs with the crème fraiche in a large bowl.
- Add the potato, garlic and rosemary, then season and mix together carefully.
- Oil a large frying pan, then pour the mixture in and bake for about 35 minutes until puffed and golden. The egg should be cooked through.
- Cut into squares and serve warm or cold.

Tomato, rosemary and potato frittata
Add a handful of chopped tomatoes or sun-dried tomatoes to the mixture before baking.

Quinoa, sweet potato and pomegranate salad

PREPARATION TIME: 30 minutes
SERVES: 2

200 g / 7 oz / 1 ¼ cups quinoa, cooked
2 sweet potatoes, skins removed, cubed and roasted
1 packet rocket (arugula) leaves
1 Hass avocado, sliced
a handful of pumpkin seeds
a handful of pomegranate seeds
2 tbsp sweetcorn, cooked
½ head broccoli, stalks removed and cooked
to al dente
2 tbsp extra-virgin olive oil
½ lemon, juiced

FOR THE AVOCADO CREAM
1 Hass avocado, flesh roughly chopped
1 tsp apple cider vinegar
1 tbsp extra-virgin olive oil
1 tbsp nutritional yeast

- Arrange the quinoa with the roasted sweet
  potato, rocket, avocado, seeds, sweetcorn and
  broccoli.
- Drizzle with olive oil and lemon juice, then
  season to taste.
- Divide the salad between each serving plate.
- For the avocado cream, simply blend the
  ingredients until smooth and spoon a little on
  each serving plate.

Feta, quinoa and pomegranate salad
Replace the sweet potato with some crumbled
feta for a tasty alternative.

Tofu sausages with braised cabbage

PREPARATION TIME: **5 minutes**
COOKING TIME: **1 hour, 15 minutes**
SERVES: **6**

2 tbsp olive oil
18 tofu sausages

FOR THE CABBAGE
2 tbsp olive oil
1 red onion, sliced
2 cloves garlic, crushed
1 red cabbage, sliced
100 ml / 3 ½ fl. oz / ½ cup port
100 ml / 3 ½ fl. oz / ½ cup red wine

- Preheat the oven to 180°C (160°C fan) / 350F / gas 4.
- Heat the oil in a cast-iron casserole dish and fry the onion and garlic for 5 minutes.
- Add the cabbage and a sprinkle of salt and pepper and sauté for 5 minutes. Pour in the port and wine, and bring to a simmer.
- Cover the dish and transfer to the oven to cook for 1 hour.
- Towards the end of the cooking time, heat the oil in a frying pan and cook the tofu sausages on both sides.
- Serve 3 sausages per person with the red cabbage on the side.

Seitan with braised cabbage
Replace the tofu sausages with 600 g/ 1 lb 5 oz marinated seitan, roughly chopped or sliced. Lightly fry the seitan pieces in a pan until cooked through.

Ratatouille with cashews

PREPARATION TIME: 10 minutes
COOKING TIME: 40 minutes
SERVES: 4

6 tbsp olive oil

2 onions, peeled and finely sliced

2 aubergines (eggplants), cut in half lengthways
and finely sliced

3 courgettes (zucchinis), cut in half lengthways
and finely sliced

2 cloves garlic, finely chopped

3 red peppers, seeded and cut into strips

a handful of black olives, pitted

roasted cashew nuts, to garnish

chives, to garnish

- Heat the oil in a pan and cook the onions
  until deep golden and sweet.
- Add the aubergines and cook for 2 minutes,
  then add the courgettes and garlic. Cook for
  2 minutes, then add the peppers and cook for
  a further 5 minutes.
- Add the olives and leave to simmer for at least
  30 minutes over a very low heat, stirring
  occasionally, until the vegetables are very
  soft.
- Season and sprinkle over the cashews and
  chives before serving.

Tomato ratatouille with cashews
Add a handful of sun-dried tomatoes and cherry
tomatoes to the pan for a rich taste. Omit the
chives and replace with some fresh basil.

Vegetarian chilli with soured cream

PREPARATION TIME: 5 minutes
COOKING TIME: 1 hour, 10 minutes
SERVES: 4

2 tbsp olive oil
1 onion, finely chopped
1 red chilli (chili), finely chopped
2 cloves of garlic, crushed
½ tsp cayenne pepper
450 g / 1 lb / 2 cups vegetarian mince
400 g / 14 oz / 1 ½ cups canned tomatoes, chopped
200 ml / 7 fl. oz / ½ cup vegetable stock
400 g / 14 oz / 1 ½ cups canned kidney beans, drained
soured cream, to serve
chopped tomatoes, to serve
fresh coriander (cilantro) leaves, to garnish

- Heat the oil in a large saucepan and fry the onion and chilli for 3 minutes, stirring occasionally.
- Add the garlic and cayenne and cook for 2 minutes, then add the vegetarian mince.
- Fry the mince until it starts to brown then add the chopped tomatoes, stock and kidney beans and bring to a gentle simmer.
- Cook the chilli con carne for 1 hour (stirring every 8-10 minutes to ensure it does not stick to the bottom of the pan) until the mince is tender and the sauce has thickened.
- Taste for seasoning and add salt and freshly ground black pepper as necessary.
- Serve with the chopped tomatoes, soured cream and coriander.

Vegan chilli with coconut yogurt
Omit the soured cream and use dairy-free coconut yogurt instead. Remember to check that the mince is vegan, if not, replace with cooked brown lentils.

Asparagus and hazelnut salad

PREPARATION TIME: 5 minutes
COOKING TIME: 25–30 minutes
SERVES: 4

2 tbsp olive oil
4 baby artichokes, halved
175 ml / 6 fl. oz / ⅔ cup dry white wine
8 shallots, peeled
500 ml / 17 ½ fl. oz / 2 cups vegetable stock
12 asparagus spears, trimmed
150 g / 5 oz / 1 cup fresh peas
8 radishes, finely sliced
4 courgettes (zucchini), spiralized or thinly sliced
1 tbsp lemon juice
2 tbsp flat-leaf parsley, finely chopped
a handful of rocket (arugula) leaves
a handful of hazelnuts (cob nuts)
feta, crumbled (optional)

- Heat the oil in a large cast-iron casserole dish and sear the cut sides of the artichokes until well browned.
- Pour in the wine and bring to the boil, then add the shallots and stock. Bring back to the boil.
- Reduce the heat and simmer gently for 10 minutes, then add the asparagus, peas, radishes and courgetti, simmering lightly for a further 8 minutes.
- Add a squeeze of lemon then season to taste with sprinkle with parsley.
- Divide the rocket between the 4 serving plates and add the mixed vegetables. Sprinkle some hazelnuts and feta on top before serving.

Quinoa spring salad
Add some cooked quinoa to the vegetables for added texture. This makes a nice light meal, suitable for summer evenings or served as a side dish.

Chestnut, sprout and mushroom stir-fry

PREPARATION TIME: **10 minutes**
COOKING TIME: **25 minutes**
SERVES: **4**

2 tbsp olive oil
1 white onion, chopped
2 cloves garlic, crushed
250 g / 9 oz Brussels sprouts, peeled and quartered
400 g / 14 oz / 2 ⅔ cups peas, defrosted if frozen
250 g / 9 oz / 1 ⅓ cups chestnut mushrooms
175 ml / 6 fl. oz / ⅔ cup dry white wine
175 ml / 6 fl. oz / ⅔ cup vegetable stock
180 g / 6 ⅓ oz / 1 ½ cups whole chestnuts (cooked), roughly chopped

- Heat the oil in a large cast-iron casserole dish and cook the onions and garlic until slightly brown.
- Add the sprouts and a little water and cook for a few minutes. Then add the peas and mushrooms and season with salt and pepper.
- Pour in the wine and bring to the boil, then add the stock and simmer for 10 minutes.
- Once the sprouts are soft, add the chestnuts and cook for a further 2 minutes. Remove the pan from the heat.
- Serve while hot.

Grainy chestnut and mushroom stir-fry
Add some cooked grains, such as pearl barley, quinoa or brown rice, for a hearty meal packed with plenty of fibre.

Sicilian caponata

PREPARATION TIME: 10 minutes
COOKING TIME: 30 minutes
SERVES: 4

4 tbsp olive oil
1 small red onion
2 cloves garlic, crushed
2 large aubergines (eggplants), cut into large chunks
5 large ripe tomatoes, roughly chopped
½ lemon, juiced
2 tbsp capers
1 tbsp pine nuts, toasted
a handful of raisins
2 tbsp herb vinegar
fresh basil leaves

- Heat a medium-sized saucepan and add 2 tablespoons of oil followed by the onions.
- Once the onions are translucent add the garlic, followed by the aubergine, tomatoes and a squeeze of lemon. Season to taste.
- Add a little water and stir regularly to help prevent the vegetables from sticking to the bottom of the pan.
- Add the remaining oil and a little more water, followed by the capers, pine nuts, raisins and vinegar.
- Add a little more water if necessary and leave to simmer for 15–20 minutes.
- Once the vegetables are soft and tender, sprinkle some fresh basil leaves on top and season to taste.

Caponata with sourdough
Add some torn sourdough bread to the caponata while cooking for a chewy, denser dish that is simply irresistible.

Butternut and kale risotto

PREPARATION TIME: 10 minutes
COOKING TIME: 35 minutes
SERVES: 4

2 tbsp olive oil
½ white onion, sliced
1 clove garlic, crushed
1 small butternut squash, peeled and cubed
½ lemon, juiced
600 ml / 1 pint 2 fl. oz / 2 ½ cups vegetable stock
200 g / 7 oz / 1 cup Arborio rice
100 ml / 3 ½ fl. oz / ½ cup white wine
a handful of kale leaves, stems removed and roughly chopped
fresh thyme, to garnish

- Warm a medium-sized frying pan over a gentle heat and add the oil, followed by the onion.
- Cook until the onion starts to turn translucent and then add the garlic and squash. Season with some salt and pepper and a squeeze of lemon.
- Add the vegetable stock, increase the heat and stir in the rice. After 5 minutes add the wine and allow the liquid to bubble before covering the pan.
- Continue to cook for 25 minutes. Add a little more water when necessary and stir every 5 minutes. Keep the lid on so the risotto retains the aromas.
- About 5 minutes before the end of the cooking time, stir in the kale leaves and sprinkle some fresh thyme. Give the risotto a stir so the leaves and herbs are evenly distributed.
- Once cooked, season to taste and divide between 4 serving plates and enjoy.

Butternut and kale spaghetti
Replace the rice with spaghetti for a satisfying alternative. Sprinkle some toasted breadcrumbs over the top for a delicious crunch.

Wild mushrooms with potato

PREPARATION TIME: 25 minutes
COOKING TIME: 12–15 minutes
SERVES: 4

4 large Maris Piper potatoes, peeled and cubed
300 g / 10 ½ oz mixed wild mushrooms
1 tbsp olive oil
2 tbsp butter
1 shallot, finely chopped
1 clove garlic, crushed
2 tbsp soured cream
2 tbsp parsley, chopped

- Boil the potatoes until tender for about 15–20 minutes. Drain the water and set to one side.
- Pick over the mushrooms and brush away any soil with a pastry brush.
- Heat the olive oil and butter in a large sauté pan until sizzling.
- Add the mushrooms and shallot, season with salt and pepper and cook for 10 minutes, stirring occasionally.
- When all the liquid that comes out of the mushrooms has evaporated and they start to brown, add the garlic and potatoes. Cook for 2 more minutes.
- Divide between 4 mini casserole dishes and top with the soured cream and a sprinkle of parsley.

Wild mushrooms with dill
Replace the parsley with some fresh dill and mix into the dish until completely incorporated. This is an ideal side dish for picnics and summer barbecues.

Sesame Asian veggies

PREPARATION TIME: 10 minutes
COOKING TIME: 6 minutes
SERVES: 4

2 tbsp sesame oil
2 cloves garlic, finely chopped
1 tbsp root ginger, finely chopped
½ Chinese cabbage, shredded
50 g / 1 ¾ oz / ⅓ cup edamame beans
50 g / 1 ¾ oz / ⅓ cup fresh sweetcorn
2 carrots, julienne
1 red chilli (chili) pepper, chopped
2 tbsp rice wine or dry sherry
1 tsp caster (superfine) sugar
1 tbsp light soy sauce
1 tbsp sesame seeds, to garnish

- Heat the oil in a large wok and fry the garlic and ginger for 30 seconds.
- Add the vegetables and stir-fry for 4 minutes.
- Mix the rice wine, sugar and soy together and add it to the wok.
- Stir-fry until the vegetables are cooked through and evenly coated with the sauce.
- Garnish with some toasted sesame seeds. Serve immediately.

Sesame Asian noodle bowl
Toss some cooked buckwheat noodles with the veggies and a little sesame oil.

Halloumi chips

PREPARATION TIME: 10 minutes
COOKING TIME: 6 minutes
SERVES: 4

oil, for deep frying
200 g / 7 oz / 1 ⅓ cups plain (all-purpose) flour
1 tbsp olive oil
250 ml / 9 fl. oz / 1 cup pale ale
1 tsp baking powder
1 block halloumi, cut into chips
tomato sauce, to serve

- Heat the oil in a deep-fat fryer, according to the manufacturer's instructions.
- To make the batter, sieve the flour into a bowl then whisk in the oil, ale and baking powder until combined. Season to taste.
- Increase the fryer temperature to 180°C / 350F. Dip the halloumi chips in the batter and fry for 6 minutes or until golden brown.
- Transfer the halloumi to a kitchen-paper-lined bowl.
- Drain the chips of excess oil and serve with the tomato sauce.

Halloumi with chips
Serve the halloumi chips alongside potato chips. Peel and cut 4 large Maris Piper potatoes into chips. Part-cook the chips for 10 minutes and then batter and fry in the deep-fat fryer for 5–10 minutes.

EVERYDAY COOKING | **VEGETARIAN**

Ricotta and spinach tray bake

PREPARATION TIME: **40 minutes**
COOKING TIME: **15 minutes**
SERVES: 3

6 cannelloni tubes

FOR THE FILLING
2 tbsp olive oil
2 cloves garlic, chopped
1 kg / 2 lb spinach leaves
½ nutmeg, grated
400 g / 14 oz ricotta
2 tbsp vegetarian Parmesan, grated

FOR THE TOMATO SAUCE
2 tbsp olive oil
1 clove garlic, chopped
2x 400 g / 14 oz cans tomatoes, chopped
½ bunch basil, chopped
1 sprig fresh oregano, chopped
½ tsp chilli (chili) flakes
½ tsp smoked paprika

- Preheat the oven to 180°C (160°C fan) / 350F / gas 4.
- To make the filling, heat the oil in a large pan and cook the garlic for 2 minutes.
- Add the spinach and nutmeg and stir until wilted.
- Spoon into a sieve and press down firmly with a wooden spoon to extract as much liquid as possible. Once done, finely chop the spinach and leave to cool in a bowl.
- Stir in the ricotta, Parmesan and seasoning.
- Spoon into the tubes, then lay in a greased baking dish.
- To make the tomato sauce, heat the oil in a pan, then add the garlic and tomatoes. Leave to simmer, topped up with a little water, for 10 minutes, then add the herbs, chilli flakes and smoked paprika.
- Spoon over the cannelloni and bake for around 15 minutes until bubbling.

Tofu and spinach tray bake
Swap out the ricotta for tofu. Simply crumble 1 block of plain or smoked tofu, mix in the spinach with some lemon juice and season to taste.

Sweet potato curry

PREPARATION TIME: 20 minutes
COOKING TIME: 12 minutes
SERVES: 4

2 medium-sized sweet potatoes, skins removed and chopped into large cubes

2 tbsp vegetable oil

2 tbsp Thai red curry paste

bunch fresh spinach, roughly chopped

400 ml / 14 fl. oz / 1 ⅔ cups coconut milk

1 tsp caster (superfine) sugar

1 large red chilli (chili), sliced

fresh coriander (cilantro) leaves, to garnish

naan bread or cooked rice, to serve

- Bring a saucepan of water to the boil and add the sweet potatoes. Cook for 15 minutes or until the potatoes are slightly soft.
- Heat the oil in a wok and fry the curry paste for 2 minutes.
- Add the spinach and sweet potatoes to the wok and stir-fry for 4 minutes then add the coconut milk and bring to a simmer.
- Simmer for 3 minutes then season to taste with the caster sugar.
- Spoon the curry onto a serving plate and garnish with chilli and coriander.
- Serve with a side of naan bread or rice.

Sweet potato and almond curry
Sprinkle some toasted almond flakes on top of the curry and serve with a side of lime pickle for an irresistible spicy kick.

Brown rice salad

PREPARATION TIME: **10 minutes**
SERVES: **4**

200 g / 7 oz / 1 ¼ cups brown basmati rice, cooked
200 g / 7 oz / 1 ⅓ cups cherry tomatoes, quartered
1 cucumber, diced
½ red onion, diced
100 g / 3 ½ oz pre-cooked beetroot, diced
4 tbsp extra-virgin olive oil
½ lemon, juiced
½ tsp ground sumac
fresh parsley leaves, chopped

• Combine the rice with the tomatoes, cucumber, onion and beetroot.
• Add the olive oil and lemon juice, sumac, parsley and season to taste.
• Mix the ingredients together to ensure the vegetables and rice are evenly coated with the oil dressing and herbs.
• Divide between 4 serving plates and enjoy.

> **Pitta and hummus salad**
> Omit the rice and serve the salad with a side of pitta and home-made hummus sprinkled with pomegranate seeds.

Salsa salad

PREPARATION TIME: **10 minutes**
SERVES: **2**

1 cucumber, chopped
1 packet rocket (arugula) leaves
1 red onion, chopped
8 cherry tomatoes, sliced
1 400 g tin red kidney beans
2 beetroots, chopped
4 tbsp extra-virgin olive oil
½ lemon, juiced
½ tsp peppercorns, crushed
1 tsp mixed herbs
1 tsp smoked paprika

• Arrange the cucumber and rocket on two plates and top with the onion, tomatoes, kidney beans, and beetroot.
• Drizzle with olive oil and lemon juice, then sprinkle with peppercorns, mixed herbs and smoked paprika.

Halloumi, bean and potato salad

PREPARATION TIME: 10 minutes
COOKING TIME: 30 minutes
SERVES: 4

800 g / 1 lb 12 oz new potatoes, halved
300 g / 10 ½ oz / 2 cups green (string) beans
iceberg lettuce, shredded
halloumi, grilled to serve

FOR THE DRESSING
1 tbsp balsamic vinegar
1 tbsp lemon juice
1 tsp runny honey
1 tsp Dijon mustard
4 tbsp olive oil
a few sprigs of parsley

- Boil the potatoes in salted water for
  25 minutes then drain well and leave to
  steam dry for 2 minutes.
- Cook the beans in boiling salted water for
  4 minutes then drain well.
- Put all the dressing ingredients in a jam jar
  with a pinch of salt and pepper then close the
  lid and shake vigorously to emulsify.
- When the potatoes are ready, toss them with
  the beans and lettuce, and enough dressing to
  lightly coat.
- Add several slices of grilled halloumi to each
  plate, then serve.

Seitan, bean and potato salad
Omit the honey and replace with maple syrup.
Then swap the grilled halloumi with cooked
seitan pieces.

Snacks and treats

Spiced maple roasted chickpeas

PREPARATION TIME: 5 minutes
COOKING TIME: 20 minutes
SERVES: 4

800 g / 1 lb 12 oz / 5 ⅓ cups canned chickpeas
(garbanzo beans)
2 tbsp olive oil
1 lime, juiced
1 tbsp smoked paprika
1 tbsp maple syrup
1 tsp chilli (chili) flakes
fresh coriander (cilantro) leaves, to garnish

- Preheat the oven to 200°C (180°C fan) / 400F
  / gas 6.
- Drain the liquid from the chickpeas and rinse
  the chickpeas thoroughly with water.
- Add the chickpeas to a baking tray with the
  oil, lime juice, paprika, maple syrup and chilli
  flakes.
- Stir well and season to taste. Transfer
  the baking tray to the oven and cook for
  20 minutes or until golden and a little crispy.
- Once cooked, garnish with some fresh
  coriander leaves and serve hot or cold.

Spiced coconut and chickpea mix
Stir in a handful of coconut flakes to the mixture
about 5 minutes before the end of cooking time.
Simply remove the baking tray from the oven
and add the dried coconut flakes, stirring well.

Date, cacao and almond energy balls

PREPARATION TIME: **10 minutes**
FREEZING TIME: **1 hour**
MAKES: **12**

200 g / 7 oz almonds
400 g / 14 oz dates, pitted
1 tbsp rolled oats
2 tbsp coconut oil
4 tbsp cacao powder
1 tbsp maple syrup
pinch sea salt
a handful of almond flakes, chopped

- Add the almonds to a food processor and pulse to a flour-like texture.
- Add the dates, oats, coconut oil, cacao and maple syrup, salt and a little water and pulse until fully combined.
- Scoop out the mixture, roll into balls and then coat with the chopped almond flakes.
- Place on a baking tray then transfer the balls to the freezer and freeze for an hour until firm.
- These energy balls can be refrigerated in an airtight container for up to 5 days.

Date, cacao and ginger energy balls
For a spicy kick, add 1 tablespoon of ground ginger or 1 tablespoon of freshly grated ginger to the mixture before blending.

Kale crisps

PREPARATION TIME: **5 minutes**
COOKING TIME: **20 minutes**
SERVES: **4**

100 g / 3 ½ oz kale, stalks removed and washed
1 tbsp olive oil
1 pinch of salt

- Heat the oven to 150°C (130°C fan)/ 300F / gas 2 and line a large baking tray with greaseproof paper.
- Combine the kale with the olive oil and a pinch of salt and gently massage the leaves.
- Bake the kale for 18–20 minutes or until the leaves are crispy.
- Leave to cool before serving.

Carrot hummus with smoked paprika

PREPARATION TIME: **15 minutes**
COOKING TIME: **30 minutes**
SERVES: **4**

3 large carrots, diced
4 tbsp olive oil
1 tbsp tahini paste
1 lemon, juiced
1 clove garlic, crushed
½ tsp smoked garlic powder
1 tsp smoked paprika
carrot sticks, for dipping

- Preheat the oven to 190°C (170°C fan) / 375F / gas 5.
- Toss the carrots with the olive oil in a large roasting tin and season with salt and pepper.
- Roast the carrots for 30 minutes or until tender, stirring halfway through.
- Transfer the carrots to a food processor with the tahini, lemon, garlic clove and smoked garlic and blend to a smooth puree.
- Season to taste with salt and pepper and then sprinkle some smoked paprika on top.
- Serve with carrot sticks for dipping.

Red pepper hummus
Replace the carrots with 1 medium-sized red pepper. Simply blend the raw red pepper with the rest of the ingredients and garnish the hummus with some chilli (chili) flakes.

Crispbread with fig and cottage cheese

PREPARATION TIME: **10 minutes**
SERVES: **8**

200 g / 7 oz / ¾ cup cottage cheese
16 wholewheat crispbreads
4 fresh figs, sliced into moon shapes
alfalfa sprouts, to garnish
honey, to drizzle

- Add a spoonful of cottage cheese to the crispbread and then layer with the fig slices and alfalfa sprouts
- Drizzle with a little honey and then serve.

Beetroot crisps

PREPARATION TIME: **35 minutes**
COOKING TIME: **6–7 minutes**
SERVES: **2–4**

250 g / 9 oz large beetroot, uncooked
2–3 litres / 3 ½–5 pints sunflower oil
sea salt for sprinkling

- Cut the beetroot into very thin slices with a mandolin slicer or sharp knife.
- Put the slices in a bowl of cold water and leave them to soak for 25 minutes to remove some of the starch.
- Drain the beetroot and dry them completely with a clean tea towel.
- Heat the oil in a deep-fat fryer, according to the manufacturer's instructions, to a temperature of 130°C / 265F.
- Lower the beetroot in the fryer basket and cook for 5 minutes so that they cook all the way through but don't brown. You may need to do this in batches so that the fryer isn't overcrowded.
- Pull up the fryer basket and increase the temperature to 190°C / 375F.
- Cook the crisps at the hotter temperature for 1–2 minutes or until crisp.
- Line a large bowl with a thick layer of kitchen paper and when the crisps are ready, tip them into the bowl to remove any excess oil.
- Leave to cool then sprinkle with sea salt.

Griddled aubergine and halloumi on sourdough

PREPARATION TIME: **5 minutes**
COOKING TIME: **8 minutes**
SERVES: **6–8**

1 tbsp olive oil
1 aubergine (eggplant), sliced into circles
200 g / 7 oz halloumi, sliced
1 loaf sourdough bread, sliced
a handful of chard salad leaves
1 lemon, juiced
½ tsp peppercorns, crushed

- Heat a griddle pan until smoking hot.
- Add the oil, aubergine and halloumi slices and cook for 4 minutes on each side on the griddle.
- Top the sourdough bread slices with the griddled aubergine, halloumi and chard leaves.
- Add a squeeze of lemon juice and some pepper, then serve.

Rocket, clementine and walnut salad

PREPARATION TIME: **10 minutes**
SERVES: **2**

1 packet rocket (arugula)
2 clementines, peeled
a handful of red grapes
a handful of walnut halves
a handful of pomegranate seeds
2 tbsp extra-virgin olive oil
½ lemon, juiced
½ tsp peppercorns, crushed
1 pinch of salt

- Combine the rocket, clementine segments, grapes, walnuts and pomegranate seeds in 2 serving bowls.
- To make the dressing, mix the olive oil, lemon juice, peppercorns and salt. Pour over the salad and mix well, then serve.

Yorkshire Cheddar pudding

PREPARATION TIME: **10 minutes**
COOKING TIME: **25 minutes**
MAKES: **2**

6 tsp cooking oil
75 g / 2 ⅔ oz / ½ cup plain (all-purpose) flour
2 large eggs
100 ml / 3 ½ fl. oz / ½ cup whole milk
1 tbsp Dijon mustard
150 g / 5 oz / 1 ½ cups Cheddar cheese, grated

- Preheat the oven to 230°C (210°C fan) / 450F / gas 8.
- Put a teaspoon of cooking oil into 2 medium-sized cast-iron pans and put them in the oven to heat.
- Put the flour in a large jug with a pinch of salt and make a well in the middle.
- Break in the eggs and pour in the milk then use a whisk to gradually incorporate all the flour from around the outside.
- Add the mustard and half of the cheese, then mix well.
- Carefully take the pans out of the oven and immediately divide the batter between each. Scatter the remaining cheese on top of the mixture.
- Return the pans to the oven and bake for 25 minutes without opening the oven door.
- Serve straight away.

Salted lemon asparagus

PREPARATION TIME: **5 minutes**
COOKING TIME: **8 minutes**
SERVES: **4**

16 asparagus spears
3 tbsp olive oil
1 pinch rock salt
freshly ground black pepper
½ lemon, juiced
½ lemon, sliced

- Heat a griddle pan until smoking hot.
- Brush the asparagus liberally with olive oil.
- Sprinkle with plenty of rock salt and black pepper, then cook for 4 minutes on each side on the griddle.
- Squeeze over the lemon juice and reserve the slices to garnish. Serve immediately.

White herby farmhouse loaf

PREPARATION TIME: **3 hours, 20 minutes**
COOKING TIME: **35–40 minutes**
MAKES: **1 loaf**

400 g / 14 oz / 2 ⅔ cups strong white bread flour, plus extra for dusting
½ tsp easy-blend dried yeast
1 tbsp caster (superfine) sugar
1 tsp fine sea salt
1 tbsp dried mixed herbs
1 tbsp olive oil
280 ml / 9 ¾ fl. oz / 1 cup warm water

- Mix together the flour, yeast, sugar, salt and herbs. Stir the oil into the warm water, then stir it into the dry ingredients.
- Knead the mixture on a lightly oiled surface for 10 minutes or until smooth and elastic.
- Leave the dough to rest in an oiled bowl, covered with oiled cling film, for 1–2 hours or until doubled in size.
- Knead for 2 more minutes then shape the dough into a long loaf on an oiled baking tray. Cover with oiled cling film and leave to prove for 1 hour or until doubled in size.
- Preheat the oven to 220°C (200°C fan) / 425F / gas 7.
- Dust the loaf with flour and score the dough down the middle and across with a knife, then transfer the tray to the top shelf of the oven. Bake for 35–40 minutes.
- Transfer to a wire rack and leave to cool.

Olive tapenade bruschetta

PREPARATION TIME: **15 minutes**
SERVES: **4**

1 ciabatta loaf, sliced
150 g / 5 oz green olive tapenade
flat-leaf parsley, to serve
cherry tomatoes on the vine, to serve
mixed olives, to serve

- Cut the bread to desired thickness and toast under a grill until crispy.
- Spread one side of each slice with tapenade.
- Garnish the bruschetta with parsley.
- Serve immediately with fresh tomatoes and olives on the side.

Black olive bruschetta
Replace the green olive tapenade with black olive tapenade, for a slightly richer flavour. Serve with a side of sun-dried tomatoes and marinated artichokes.

Summer salad and feta bruschetta

PREPARATION TIME: **15 minutes**
SERVES: **8**

1 ciabatta loaf, sliced
a handful of lettuce leaves
1 red onion, diced
1 red pepper, diced
1 yellow pepper, diced
½ cucumber, diced
a handful of black olives, pitted and sliced
200 g / 7 oz feta, crumbled
fresh parsley, to garnish
½ lemon, juiced
½ tsp peppercorns, crushed
1 pinch salt

- Slice and lightly toast the ciabatta under the grill.
- Top the ciabatta slices with the lettuce leaves, onion, pepper, cucumber, olives, feta and parsley.
- Add a squeeze of lemon juice, some pepper and a pinch of salt, then serve.

Sesame soya rolls

PREPARATION TIME: **20 minutes**
COOKING TIME: **25 minutes**
MAKES: **6**

350 g / 12 oz soya meat
1 small onion, grated
1 small apple, grated
500 g / 1 lb 2 oz all-butter puff pastry
1 egg, beaten
1 tbsp sesame seeds

- Preheat the oven to 230°C (210°C fan) / 450F / gas 8.
- Mix the soya meat with the onion and apple and season with salt and pepper.
- Roll out the pastry on a lightly floured surface into a large rectangle and cut in half lengthways.
- Shape the soya meat into 2 long sausages the length of the pastry strips, then fold over the pastry to enclose.
- Seal the edge with beaten egg and score at 1 cm (½ in) intervals with a sharp knife. Cut each roll into 3 equal pieces and transfer them to a baking tray.
- Brush the tops with beaten egg and sprinkle with sesame seeds, then bake for 25 minutes or until golden brown and cooked through.

Poppy seed soya rolls
Replace the sesame seeds for the same quantity of poppy seeds for a delicious alternative.

Rainbow salad wrap

PREPARATION TIME: **10 minutes**
SERVES: **4**

½ cucumber, julienne
1 carrot, julienne
a handful of green olives, pitted
4 flour tortillas
a handful of fresh coriander (cilantro), to garnish
½ lime, juiced

- Divide all the ingredients between the 4 tortillas and season with salt and black pepper.
- Add a few leaves of coriander and a splash of fresh lime juice. Season to taste, then serve immediately.

Garlic new potatoes

PREPARATION TIME: 10 minutes
COOKING TIME: 45–50 minutes
SERVES: 4

800 g / 1 lb 12 oz baby new potatoes
6 tbsp olive oil
2 cloves garlic, crushed
1 tsp garlic powder
Szechuan pepper
rosemary salt
a handful of flat-leaf parsley, chopped

- Preheat the oven to 200°C (180°C fan) / 400F / gas 6.
- Boil the potatoes in salted water for 10 minutes then drain well and leave to steam dry for 2 minutes.
- Put the oil in a large roasting tin in the oven to heat for 2 minutes.
- Add the potatoes, crushed garlic and garlic powder to the roasting tin and stir to coat in the oil.
- Roast the potatoes for 45 minutes or until golden brown then sprinkle with Szechuan pepper and rosemary salt.
- Garnish with the parsley, before serving.

Turmeric mango smoothie

PREPARATION TIME: **10 minutes**
SERVES: **4**

400 ml / 14 fl. oz / 1 ⅔ cups almond milk
4 bananas, chopped
1 large mango, roughly chopped with skins and stone removed
2 tbsp almond butter
1 tsp ground or fresh turmeric
4 dates, stones removed
a handful of ice
cinnamon stick, to garnish

- Whizz the milk, banana, chopped mango, almond butter, turmeric, dates and a handful of ice in a blender, according to the manufacturer's instructions.
- Garnish with a cinnamon stick.
- Serve cold.

Chai smoothie
Replace the turmeric with 1 teaspoon of ground cinnamon and 1 teaspoon of ground ginger before blending. Grate some fresh nutmeg on top, to garnish.

Spicy lemon wedges

PREPARATION TIME: **10 minutes**
COOKING TIME: **35–40 minutes**
SERVES: **4**

4 tbsp olive oil
800 g / 1 lb 12 oz potatoes, cut into wedges
1 tbsp chilli (chili) flakes
1 tsp smoked paprika
1 lemon, juiced
1 pinch smoked salt
freshly ground black pepper
a handful of fresh coriander (cilantro) leaves, chopped

- Preheat the oven to 220°C (200°C fan) / 425F / gas 7.
- Put the oil in a large roasting tin and heat in the oven for 5 minutes.
- Carefully tip the potato wedges into the pan and turn to coat in the oil. Add the chilli, paprika, lemon juice and smoked salt. Mix well then season with black pepper.
- Bake the wedges for 35–40 minutes, turning them every 15 minutes, until golden brown on the outside and fluffy within.
- Sprinkle with a little more smoked salt and fresh coriander. Serve hot or cold.

Raisin and fig scones

PREPARATION TIME: 10 minutes
COOKING TIME: 10–15 minutes
MAKES: 12

225 g / 8 oz / 1 ½ cups self-raising flour
55 g / 2 oz / ¼ cup butter
75 g / 2 ⅔ oz / ⅓ cup raisins
75 g / 2 ⅔ oz / ⅓ cup dried figs, chopped
150 ml / 5 ⅓ fl. oz / ⅔ cup milk
plain yogurt, to serve

- Preheat the oven to 220°C (200°C fan) / 425F / gas 7 and oil a large baking sheet.
- Sieve the flour into a bowl and rub in the butter until the mixture resembles fine breadcrumbs.
- Add the raisins and figs and stir in enough milk to bring the mixture together into a soft dough.
- Flatten the dough with your hands on a floured work surface until 2.5 cm (1 in) thick.
- Use a pastry cutter to cut out 12 scones and transfer them to the prepared baking sheet.
- Bake in the oven for 10–15 minutes or until golden brown and cooked through.
- Transfer the scones to a wire rack to cool a little.
- Serve warm with plain yogurt on the side.

Cranberry and raisin scones
Replace the dried figs with the same amount of dried cranberries.

Nutty banana bread

PREPARATION TIME: 10 minutes
COOKING TIME: 50–55 minutes
MAKES: 1 loaf

3 very ripe bananas
100 g / 3 ½ oz / ½ cup soft light brown sugar
2 large eggs
125 ml / 4 ⅓ fl. oz / ½ cup sunflower oil
2 tbsp crunchy peanut butter
225 g / 8 oz / 1 ½ cups plain (all-purpose) flour
1 tsp bicarbonate of (baking) soda
75 g / 2 ⅔ oz / ⅔ cup mixed nuts, chopped

- Preheat the oven to 160°C (140°C fan) / 325F / gas 3 and line a loaf tin with greaseproof paper.
- Mash the bananas roughly with a fork then whisk in the sugar, eggs, oil and peanut butter.
- Sieve the flour and bicarbonate of soda into the bowl and add the chopped nuts. Stir just enough to evenly mix all the ingredients together.
- Scrape the mixture into the loaf tin and bake for 50–55 minutes or until a skewer inserted into the middle comes out clean.
- Transfer the banana bread to a wire rack and leave to cool completely.

Spiced walnut loaf

PREPARATION TIME: **3 hours, 30 minutes**
COOKING TIME: **35–40 minutes**
MAKES: **1 loaf**

200 g / 7 oz / 1 ⅓ cups strong white bread flour, plus extra for dusting
200 g / 7 oz / 1 ⅓ cups stone-ground wholemeal flour
½ tsp easy-blend dried yeast
1 tbsp caster (superfine) sugar
200 g / 7 oz / 1 ⅔ cups walnut pieces
1 tsp fine sea salt
½ tsp ground ginger
½ tsp ground nutmeg
½ tsp ground star anise
½ tsp ground cardamom
½ tsp ground cinnamon
1 tbsp sunflower oil
280 ml / 9 ¾ fl. oz / 1 cup warm water

- Mix together the flours, yeast, sugar, walnuts, salt and spices. Stir the oil into the warm water and stir it into the bowl.
- Knead on a lightly oiled surface for 10 minutes or until the dough is smooth and elastic. Leave the dough to rest, covered with oiled cling film, for 1–2 hours or until doubled in size. Then, knead the dough for 2 more minutes, then shape it into a loaf.
- Transfer to a greased baking tray and cover. Leave to prove for 1 hour or until doubled in size.
- Meanwhile, preheat the oven to 220°C (200°C fan) / 425F / gas 7. When the dough has risen, slash the top with a sharp knife. Transfer the tray to the top shelf of the oven then bake for 35–40 minutes or until the loaf sounds hollow when tapped.

Trail mix apple slices

PREPARATION TIME: **10 minutes**
SERVES: **4**

4 tbsp smooth peanut butter
2 large red apples, sliced into discs and seeds removed
a handful of flaked almonds
a handful of dark chocolate chips
a handful of white chocolate chips
a handful of chopped pecans

- Spread a generous layer of peanut butter on the apple disc and then sprinkle the remaining ingredients on top.
- Enjoy as a snack between meals or as a simple dessert.

Pear and ginger loaf cake

PREPARATION TIME: 15 minutes
COOKING TIME: 50–55 minutes
MAKES: 1 loaf

300 g / 10 ½ oz / 2 cups self-raising flour
2 tsp baking powder
250 g / 9 oz / 1 ¼ cups caster (superfine) sugar
1 tsp ground ginger
1 tbsp fresh ginger, peeled and grated
250 g / 9 oz / 1 ¼ cups butter, softened
6 large eggs
2 ripe pears, peeled and chopped
1 ripe pear, halved

- Preheat the oven to 160°C (140°C fan) / 325F / gas 3 and line a large loaf tin with greaseproof paper.
- Sieve the flour and baking powder into a mixing bowl and add the sugar, ground ginger, grated ginger, butter and eggs.
- Beat the mixture with an electric whisk for 4 minutes or until smooth then fold in the chopped pears.
- Place the 2 pear halves at the ends of the tin (narrow side), with the flat side against the tin.
- Spoon the mixture into the tin and level the top with a spatula.
- Bake for 50–55 minutes or until a skewer inserted comes out clean.
- Transfer the loaf to a wire rack and leave to cool completely before slicing.

Spiced winter loaf

PREPARATION TIME: 3 hours
COOKING TIME: 35–40 minutes
MAKES: 1 loaf

55 g / 2 oz / ¼ cup butter, cubed

400 g / 14 oz / 2 ⅔ cups strong white bread flour, plus extra for dusting

½ tsp easy-blend dried yeast

4 tbsp caster (superfine) sugar

1 tsp fine sea salt

2 tsp mixed spice

1 tsp ground vanilla

100 g / 3 ½ oz / ½ cup raisins

1 egg, beaten

250 ml / 9 fl. oz / 1 cup warm water

icing (confectioners') sugar, to dust

- Rub the butter into the bread flour and stir in the yeast, sugar, salt, spice and vanilla. Stir the raisins and egg into the warm water and stir into the dry ingredients.
- Knead on a lightly oiled surface for 10 minutes.
- Leave the dough to rest, covered with a lightly oiled bowl, for 1–2 hours or until doubled in size.
- Dust the work surface with icing sugar and press the dough out into a rectangle.
- Transfer the loaf to a greased baking tray and leave to prove, covered, for 45 minutes.
- Preheat the oven to 220°C (200°C fan) / 425F / gas 7.
- Bake for 35–40 minutes or until the underneath sounds hollow when tapped.
- Leave to cool completely on a wire rack then dust liberally with icing sugar.

Spiced stollen

Add 250 g / 9 oz marzipan to the middle of the cake dough before rolling into a rectangle shape for a traditional stolen recipe. Bake as normal.

Sesame, cinnamon and honey bites

PREPARATION TIME: **10 minutes**
COOKING TIME: **12–15 minutes**
MAKES: **12**

75 g / 2 ⅔ oz / ⅓ cup butter, cubed
150 g / 5 oz / 1 cup self-raising flour, plus extra for dusting
100 g / 3 ½ oz / ⅔ cup wholemeal flour
1 ½ tbsp ground cinnamon
150 ml / 5 ⅓ fl. oz / ⅔ cup milk, plus extra for brushing
4 tbsp runny honey
4 tbsp sesame seeds

- Preheat the oven to 220°C (200°C fan) / 425F / gas 7 and line a baking tray with greaseproof paper.
- Rub the butter into the flours with your fingertips until the mixture resembles fine breadcrumbs.
- Add the cinnamon then pour in the milk and honey and mix together into a dough.
- Turn the dough out onto a floured work surface and press it out into a rectangle, 2 cm (1 in) thick.
- Use a round pastry cutter to stamp out the bites and transfer them to the baking tray.
- Brush with milk and sprinkle with sesame seeds then bake for 12–15 minutes or until golden brown and cooked through.
- Transfer the bites to a wire rack to cool a little before serving.

Home-made raisin buns

PREPARATION TIME: 3 hours
COOKING TIME: 15–20 minutes
MAKES: 12

55 g / 2 oz / ¼ cup butter, cubed
400 g / 14 oz / 2 ⅔ cups strong white bread flour, plus extra for dusting
½ tsp easy-blend dried yeast
4 tbsp caster (superfine) sugar
1 tsp fine sea salt
½ tsp mixed spice
100 g / 3 ½ oz / ½ cup raisins
280 ml / 9 ¾ fl. oz / 1 cup warm water
softened butter, for spreading

- Rub the butter into the flour and stir in the yeast, sugar, salt, spice and raisins.
- Add the dry ingredients to the warm water and combine into a dough.
- Knead on a lightly oiled surface for 10 minutes or until the dough is smooth and elastic.
- Leave the dough to rest, covered with the mixing bowl, for 1–2 hours or until doubled in size.
- Shape the dough into 12 buns and transfer to a greased baking tray, then cover and leave to prove for 45 minutes.
- Preheat the oven to 220°C (200°C fan) / 425F / gas 7.
- Bake the buns for 15–20 minutes or until golden brown and cooked through.
- Leave to cool on a wire rack then split in half and toast under a hot grill. Spread with butter before serving.

Mixed fruit tea cakes
Replace the raisins with the same quantity of mixed fruit and soak the fruit in a bowl of freshly brewed tea for 20 minutes, before combining with the flour mixture.

Chocolate and ginger cake

PREPARATION TIME: 15 minutes
COOKING TIME: 35–40 minutes
SERVES: 8

250 g / 9 oz / 1 ⅔ cups self-raising flour
1 tsp bicarbonate of (baking) soda
2 tbsp unsweetened cocoa powder
1 tbsp ground ginger
200 g / 7 oz / ⅔ cup maple syrup
125 g / 4 ⅓ oz / ½ cup butter
125 g / 4 ⅓ oz / ¾ cup dark brown sugar
2 large eggs, beaten
240 ml / 8 ½ fl. oz / 1 cup milk

- Preheat the oven to 180°C (160°C fan) / 350F / gas 4 and grease and line a 23 cm (9 in) round cake tin.
- Sieve the flour, bicarbonate of soda, cocoa and ground ginger into a bowl.
- Put the maple syrup, butter and brown sugar in a small saucepan and boil gently for 2 minutes, stirring to dissolve the sugar.
- Add the butter and sugar mixture to the flour with the eggs and milk and fold it all together until smooth.
- Scrape the mixture into the prepared tin and bake for 35–40 minutes. The cake is ready when a toothpick inserted comes out with just a few sticky crumbs clinging to it.
- Transfer the cake to a wire rack to cool completely.

Chocolate and vanilla cake
Replace the ground ginger with 1 teaspoon of vanilla powder and 3 drops of vanilla essence. Add with the wet ingredients before folding together.

Apple and blackcurrant charlotte cake

PREPARATION TIME: **20 minutes**
COOKING TIME: **30 minutes**
SERVES: **10**

3 Bramley apples, peeled, cored and cubed
75 g / 2 ⅔ oz / ½ cup blackcurrants
100 g / 3 ½ oz / ½ cup brown sugar
½ tsp mixed spice
1 lemon, zest finely grated
75 g / 2 ⅔ oz / ⅓ cup butter, softened
1 loaf white bread, sliced and crusts removed
icing (confectioners') sugar, to sieve on top

- Preheat the oven to 180°C (160°C fan) / 350F / gas 4.
- Mix the apples and blackcurrants with the sugar, spice and lemon zest in a saucepan then cook, covered, over a medium heat for 8 minutes, stirring occasionally.
- Butter the bread and cut each slice into quarters.
- Line a deep 20 cm (8 in) round spring-form cake tin with some of the bread and fill with half of the apple and blackcurrants.
- Top with more bread slices and spoon in the rest of the fruit before adding a final layer of bread.
- Bake the charlotte for 30 minutes or until the top is golden brown. Unmould the cake and cut into wedges, then sieve over some icing sugar.

Maple apple charlotte cake
Add 100 g / 3 ½ oz / ⅓ cup maple syrup and 100 ml / 3 ½ fl. oz / ½ cup double (heavy) cream to a small saucepan and stir over a low heat. Bring to the boil then remove from the heat and chill the sauce for 1 hour to thicken. Serve with the cake.

Fudgy peppermint chocolate cake

PREPARATION TIME: 15 minutes
COOKING TIME: 30 minutes
SERVES: 8

200 g / 7 oz / 1 ⅓ cups self-raising flour
225 g / 8 oz / 2 ¼ cups ground almonds
2 tbsp unsweetened cocoa powder, plus extra for dusting
1 tbsp bicarbonate of (baking) soda
225 g / 8 oz / 1 cup caster (superfine) sugar
2 tbsp golden syrup
3 large eggs, beaten
150 ml / 5 ⅓ fl. oz / ⅔ cup sunflower oil
150 ml / 5 ⅓ fl. oz / ⅔ cup semi-skimmed milk
fresh mint leaves, to garnish

FOR THE TOPPING
75 g / 2 ⅔ oz / ⅓ cup unsalted butter
175 g / 6 oz / 1 ¾ cups icing (confectioners') sugar
3 tbsp cocoa powder
3 drops peppermint extract
2–3 tbsp milk

- Preheat the oven to 200°C (180°C fan) / 400F / gas 6. Grease and line two 18 cm (7 in) sandwich tins.
- Sieve the flour, ground almonds, cocoa powder and bicarbonate of soda into a bowl. Add the sugar and mix well.
- Make a well in the middle and add the syrup, eggs, oil and milk. Beat well using an electric whisk until all the ingredients are fully incorporated.
- Divide the mixture between the 2 tins and bake for 25–30 minutes until risen and springy to touch. Remove from the oven and transfer onto a wire rack to cool.
- To make the fudgy icing, place the butter in a bowl and beat until soft. Slowly sift and beat the icing sugar and cocoa powder then add the peppermint extract and enough milk so the icing is fluffy and spreadable.
- Sandwich the 2 halves together with the icing and cover the top of the cake with the remaining icing.
- Garnish with some fresh mint leaves and serve.

Orange chocolate cake
Replace the peppermint extract with a few drops of orange extract. To garnish, sprinkle the zest of 1 orange on top of the cake for a zesty finish.

Pecan and ginger maple cheesecake

PREPARATION TIME: **20 minutes**
COOKING TIME: **40 minutes**
CHILLING TIME: **2 hours**
SERVES: **8**

200 g / 7 oz ginger biscuits, crushed
50 g / 1 ¾ oz / ¼ cup butter, melted
600 g / 1 lb 5 oz / 2 ½ cups cream cheese
150 ml / 5 ⅓ fl. oz / ⅔ cup soured cream
2 large eggs, plus 1 egg yolk
2 tbsp plain (all-purpose) flour
100 ml / 3 ½ fl. oz / ⅓ cup maple syrup
75 g / 2 ⅔ oz / ⅓ cup caster (superfine) sugar

FOR THE PECAN TOPPING
3 tbsp maple syrup
180 g / 6 ½ oz dates
½ tsp ground ginger
75 g / 2 ⅔ oz / ⅔ cup pecan nuts

- Preheat the oven to 180°C (160°C fan) / 350F / gas 4 and grease a 23 cm (9 in) round spring-form cake tin.
- Mix the biscuit crumbs with the butter and press into an even layer in the bottom of the tin.
- Bake the biscuit layer for 5 minutes or until firm.
- Whisk together the cream cheese, soured cream, eggs, egg yolk and flour until smooth. Divide the mixture between 2 bowls and beat the maple syrup into one half. Pour it into the tin and level the surface.
- Beat the caster sugar into the second bowl, then spoon it into the tin and level the surface.
- Bake the cheesecake for 40 minutes. Leave to cool completely in the tin then chill for 2 hours.
- To make the topping, simply blend the maple syrup, dates, ginger and a little water until smooth. Add a little more water if necessary.
- Once the cheesecake is set, spread the topping evenly across the top and add some pecans for decoration.

Pecan and vanilla maple cheesecake
Replace the ginger nut biscuits with digestives and for the topping, swap the ground ginger with the same amount of ground vanilla powder. Add 3 drops of vanilla essence to the cream cheese mixture before whisking.

Chocolate raspberry Victoria sponge

PREPARATION TIME: 10 minutes
COOKING TIME: 35–40 minutes
SERVES: 10

200 g / 7 oz / 1 ⅓ cups self-raising flour
200 g / 7 oz / ¾ cup caster (superfine) sugar
200 g / 7 oz / ¾ cup butter
4 large eggs
1 tsp baking powder
2 tsp vanilla extract
2 tbsp unsweetened cocoa powder

FOR THE MIDDLE
100 g / 3 ½ oz / ½ cup butter, softened
200 g / 7 oz / 2 cups icing (confectioners') sugar, plus extra for dusting
300 g / 10 ½ oz / 1 ¼ cups raspberry jam (jelly)
1 punnet fresh raspberries, washed

- Preheat the oven to 180°C (160°C fan) / 350F / gas 4 and line two 20 cm (8 in) round loose-bottomed cake tins.
- Put all the cake ingredients in a large mixing bowl and whisk until pale and well whipped.
- Divide the mixture between the 2 tins and level the tops with a spatula.
- Bake for 35–40 minutes. The cakes are ready when a toothpick inserted comes out clean.
- Transfer the cakes to a wire rack to cool completely.
- To make the buttercream, whisk the butter with an electric whisk then gradually add the icing sugar. Whisk until smooth and well whipped. If the mixture is too stiff add a tablespoon of warm water.
- Spread the raspberry jam onto one of the cakes with a palette knife and top with the buttercream and fresh raspberries.
- Place the second cake on top and dust with icing sugar.

Chocolate strawberry Victoria sponge
Swap the fresh raspberries with fresh strawberries and use strawberry jam (jelly) instead.

Cinnamon sugar waffle biscuits

PREPARATION TIME: **10 minutes**
COOKING TIME: **30–35 minutes**
MAKES: **36**

110 g / 4 oz / ½ cup butter, softened
3 large eggs, beaten
150 g / 5 oz / ⅔ cup caster (superfine) sugar
2 tsp baking powder
225 g / 8 oz / 1 ½ cups self-raising flour
1 sprig fresh mint

FOR THE CINNAMON SUGAR
50 g / 1 ¾ oz / ¼ cup granulated white or brown sugar
1 tbsp ground cinnamon

- Beat all the ingredients together until smooth.
- Heat a pizzelle iron on the hob until very hot, then add a heaped teaspoon of batter to each waffle indent and close the 2 halves together.
- Cook the waffles for 30 seconds to 1 minute or until cooked through.
- Keep the cooked waffles warm in a low oven as you cook all 36 waffles.
- To make the cinnamon sugar, simply combine the sugar with the cinnamon.
- Dust the waffles with the cinnamon sugar and serve in a cone with a sprig of mint to garnish.

Lemon vanilla madeira cake

PREPARATION TIME: **10 minutes**
COOKING TIME: **55 minutes**
SERVES: **8**

200 g / 7 oz / 1 ⅓ cups self-raising flour, sifted
50 g / 1 ¾ oz / ½ cup ground almonds
175 g / 6 oz / ¾ cup caster (superfine) sugar
175 g / 6 oz / ¾ cup butter, softened
1 tbsp ground vanilla
3 large eggs
1 lemon, zest finely grated
icing (confectioners') sugar, to serve

- Preheat the oven to 160°C (140°C fan) / 325F / gas 3 and line a large loaf tin with greaseproof paper.
- Combine the flour, ground almonds, sugar, butter, vanilla, eggs and lemon zest in a bowl and whisk together for 2 minutes or until smooth.
- Scrape the mixture into the tin and level the top then bake for 55 minutes or until a toothpick inserted comes out clean.
- Transfer to a wire rack and leave to cool completely. Sieve over some icing sugar before serving.

Prune and walnut muffins

PREPARATION TIME: 10 minutes
COOKING TIME: 15–20 minutes
MAKES: 12

1 tbsp coconut oil, melted
110 g / 4 oz / ⅔ cup wholemeal flour, sifted
110 g / 4 oz / ⅔ cup plain (all-purpose) flour, sifted
110 g / 4 oz / ½ cup caster (superfine) sugar
3 tsp baking powder
110 g / 4 oz / ½ cup butter, softened
2 large eggs
75 g / 2 ⅔ oz / ⅔ cup walnuts, chopped
36 prunes, stoned and roughly chopped

• Preheat the oven to 190°C (170°C fan) / 375F / gas 5 and grease a 12-hole silicone muffin mould with coconut oil.
• Combine the flour, sugar, baking powder, butter, eggs, half of the walnuts and prunes in a bowl and whisk together for 2 minutes or until smooth.
• Divide the mixture between the moulds and top with the remaining walnuts. Bake for 15–20 minutes.
• Test with a wooden toothpick, if it comes out clean, the muffins are done.

Prune and pecan muffins
Replace the walnuts with the same amount of roughly chopped pecans. Follow the same method, reserving some of the pecans for the topping.

Vanilla and almond muffins

PREPARATION TIME: **10 minutes**
COOKING TIME: **20–25 minutes**
MAKES: **12**

1 large egg
120 ml / 4 ¼ fl. oz / ½ cup sunflower oil
120 ml / 4 ¼ fl. oz / ½ cup milk
375 g / 13 oz / 2 ½ cups self-raising flour, sifted
1 tsp baking powder
200 g / 7 oz / ¾ cup caster (superfine) sugar
2 drops vanilla essence
1 tsp vanilla powder
4 tbsp flaked (slivered) almonds

- Preheat the oven to 180°C (160°C fan) / 350F / gas 4 and oil a 12-hole silicone muffin mould.
- Beat the egg in a jug with the oil and milk until well mixed.
- Mix together the flour, baking powder, sugar, vanilla essence, vanilla powder and half of the almonds, then pour in the egg mixture and stir just enough to combine.
- Spoon the mixture into the mould, sprinkle with the remaining almonds then bake in the oven for 20–25 minutes.
- Test with a wooden toothpick, if it comes out clean, the muffins are done.
- Transfer the muffins to a wire rack and leave to cool completely.

Almond and coconut muffins
Replace the vanilla essence and powder with desiccated coconut. Simply add 4 tablespoons of desiccated coconut to the wet ingredients and mix well before baking.

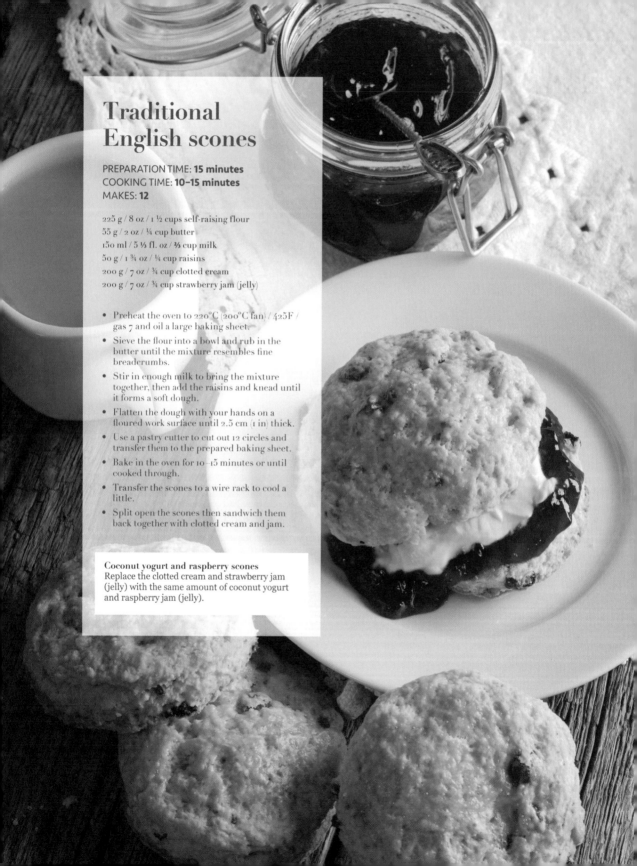

Traditional English scones

PREPARATION TIME: **15 minutes**
COOKING TIME: **10–15 minutes**
MAKES: **12**

225 g / 8 oz / 1 ½ cups self-raising flour
55 g / 2 oz / ¼ cup butter
150 ml / 5 ⅓ fl. oz / ⅔ cup milk
50 g / 1 ¾ oz / ¼ cup raisins
200 g / 7 oz / ¾ cup clotted cream
200 g / 7 oz / ¾ cup strawberry jam (jelly)

- Preheat the oven to 220°C (200°C fan) / 425F / gas 7 and oil a large baking sheet.
- Sieve the flour into a bowl and rub in the butter until the mixture resembles fine breadcrumbs.
- Stir in enough milk to bring the mixture together, then add the raisins and knead until it forms a soft dough.
- Flatten the dough with your hands on a floured work surface until 2.5 cm (1 in) thick.
- Use a pastry cutter to cut out 12 circles and transfer them to the prepared baking sheet.
- Bake in the oven for 10–15 minutes or until cooked through.
- Transfer the scones to a wire rack to cool a little.
- Split open the scones then sandwich them back together with clotted cream and jam.

Coconut yogurt and raspberry scones
Replace the clotted cream and strawberry jam (jelly) with the same amount of coconut yogurt and raspberry jam (jelly).

Matcha chia pudding

PREPARATION TIME: **10 minutes**
SERVES: **2**

1 large Hass avocado
100 ml / 3 ½ fl. oz / ½ cup coconut yogurt
1 lime, juiced
2 tbsp chia seeds
2 tbsp maple syrup
1 tsp matcha powder
1 strawberry, quartered
1 sprig fresh mint

- Remove the stone from the avocado and scoop out the flesh.
- Add the avocado, yogurt, lime juice, chia seeds, maple syrup and matcha powder to a blender. Blitz until smooth and creamy. Add some water if necessary.
- Spoon the pudding into serving glasses and garnish with the strawberry slices and a sprig of mint.

Fruit salad with mint

PREPARATION TIME: **10 minutes**
SERVES: **2**

1 honeydew melon, skins removed and chopped into large chunks
2 nectarines, stones removed and chopped into chunks
200 g / 7 oz / 1 ⅓ cups seedless green grapes
100 g / 3 ½ oz / ⅔ cup blueberries
100 g / 3 ½ oz / ⅔ cup blackberries
100 g / 3 ½ oz / ⅔ cup raspberries
fresh mint, to garnish

- Mix everything carefully together then divide it between the 2 serving bowls.
- Garnish the tops with sprigs of mint before serving.

Fruit salad and coconut yogurt
Serve the salad with some coconut yogurt for a delicious, healthy breakfast or dessert.

Zesty orange mince pies

PREPARATION TIME: 1 hour
COOKING TIME: 12–15 minutes
MAKES: 12

150 g / 5 oz / ⅔ cup butter, cubed and chilled
300 g / 10 ½ oz / 2 cups plain (all-purpose) flour
225 g / 8 oz / 1 cup mincemeat
3 large oranges, juiced and zested
1 egg, beaten
icing (confectioners') sugar, to dust

- Rub the butter into the flour until the mixture resembles fine breadcrumbs. Stir in just enough cold water to bring the pastry together into a dough.
- Leave the pastry to chill in the fridge for 30 minutes.
- Preheat the oven to 200°C (180°C fan) / 400F / gas 6.
- Roll out the pastry on a floured surface and cut out 24 circles. Use 12 of the circles to line a 12-hole cupcake tin and cut a star out of the middle of the other 12 circles.
- Combine the mincemeat with the orange juice and zest. Then fill with mincemeat then top with the pastry stars, sealing the edges with a little beaten egg.
- Brush the pies with egg then bake for 12–15 minutes.
- Once cooked, dust with a little icing sugar and enjoy hot or cold.

Classic fruit cake

PREPARATION TIME: **10 minutes**
COOKING TIME: **35–40 minutes**
SERVES: **8**

175 g / 6 oz / 1 ¼ cups self-raising flour, sifted
1 tsp baking powder
175 g / 6 oz / ¾ cup caster (superfine) sugar
175 g / 6 oz / ¾ cup butter, softened
3 large eggs
1 lemon, zest finely grated
1 orange, zest finely grated
100 g / 3 ½ oz / ½ cup dried mixed fruit
icing (confectioners') sugar, for dusting

- Preheat the oven to 180°C (160°C fan) / 350F / gas 4 and oil and line a 23 cm (9 in) round cake tin with greaseproof paper.
- Combine the flour, baking powder, sugar, butter, eggs, lemon and orange zest and dried fruit in a bowl and whisk together for 2 minutes or until smooth.
- Scrape the mixture into the tin and level the top then bake for 35–40 minutes or until a toothpick inserted comes out clean.
- Transfer the cake to a wire rack and leave to cool completely, then remove the greaseproof paper and dust lightly with icing sugar.

Ginger walnut tart

PREPARATION TIME: **40 minutes**
COOKING TIME: **45 minutes**
SERVES: **4**

400 g / 14 oz / 2 ⅓ cups dark brown sugar
200 g / 7 oz / ⅔ cup golden syrup
200 g / 7 oz / ¾ cup butter
2 tsp ground ginger
6 large eggs, beaten
300 g / 10 ½ oz walnut halves

FOR THE PASTRY
150 g / 5 oz / ⅔ cup butter, cubed and chilled
300 g / 10 ½ oz / 2 cups plain (all-purpose) flour

- Begin by making the pastry. Rub the butter into the flour then add just enough cold water to bind the mixture together into a dough.
- Roll out the pastry on a floured surface and use it to line a large round tart case then chill in the fridge for 30 minutes.
- Preheat the oven to 180°C (160°C fan) / 350F / gas 4.
- Put the sugar, golden syrup, butter and ground ginger in a saucepan and stir it over a low heat to dissolve the sugar.
- Leave the mixture to cool for 10 minutes then beat in the eggs.
- Pour the mixture into the chilled pastry case and arrange the walnuts on top, then bake the tart for 45–50 minutes.

Raspberry sponge cake

PREPARATION TIME: **15 minutes**
COOKING TIME: **25 minutes**
SERVES: **6**

100 g / 3 ½ oz / ⅔ cup self-raising flour
1 tsp baking powder
100 g / 3 ½ oz / ½ cup caster (superfine) sugar
100 g / 3 ½ oz / ½ cup butter, softened
2 large eggs
4 tbsp raspberry jam (jelly)
250 g / 9 oz / 1 ⅔ cups fresh raspberries
icing (confectioners') sugar, for dusting

- Preheat the oven to 180°C (160°C fan) / 350F / gas 4 and butter a 20 cm (8 in) round cake tin.
- Sieve the flour and baking powder into a mixing bowl and add sugar, butter and eggs.
- Beat the mixture with an electric whisk for 4 minutes or until smooth and well whipped.
- Spoon the cake mixture into the prepared tin and level with a palette knife. Bake for 25 minutes or until a skewer inserted comes out clean.
- Leave the cake to cool before turning out onto a serving plate.
- To decorate, spread the jam evenly on the cake and then place the fresh raspberries on top. Sprinkle with icing sugar just before serving.

Blueberry sponge cake
For a different berry variation on this deliciously simple cake, replace the raspberry jam (jelly) and fresh raspberries with the same amount of blueberry jam (jelly) and fresh blueberries.

Sultana scones

PREPARATION TIME: 20 minutes
COOKING TIME: 10–15 minutes
MAKES: 12

55 g / 2 oz / ¼ cup butter
225 g / 8 oz / 1 ½ cups self-raising wholemeal flour
75 g / 2 ⅔ oz / ⅓ cup sultanas
150 ml / 5 ⅓ fl. oz / ⅔ cup milk
200 g / 7 oz / ¾ cup clotted cream
200 g / 7 oz / ¾ cup raspberry jam (jelly)

- Preheat the oven to 220°C (200°C fan) / 425F / gas 7 and oil a large baking sheet.
- Rub the butter into the flour until the mixture resembles fine breadcrumbs.
- Add the sultanas then stir in enough milk to bring the mixture together into a soft dough.
- Flatten the dough with your hands on a floured work surface until 2.5 cm (1 in) thick.
- Use a pastry cutter to cut out 12 circles and transfer them to the prepared baking sheet.
- Bake in the oven for 10–15 minutes or until golden brown and cooked through.
- Transfer the scones to a wire rack to cool a little.
- Split open the scones then sandwich them back together with clotted cream and jam.

Cranberry scones
Replace the sultanas for the same amount of dried cranberries for a scrummy alternative.

Blueberry and banana smoothie

PREPARATION TIME: 10 minutes
SERVES: 4

400 ml / 14 fl. oz / 1 ⅔ cups almond milk
4 bananas, chopped
1 tbsp acai powder
a handful of blueberries (fresh or frozen)
a handful of ice cubes

- Whizz the milk, banana, acai powder, blueberries and a handful of ice cubes in a blender, according to the manufacturer's instructions.
- Garnish with some fresh blueberries and serve cold.

Hot chocolate marble cake

PREPARATION TIME: 10 minutes
COOKING TIME: 40–50 minutes
SERVES: 8

100 g / 3 ½ oz / ⅔ cup self-raising flour
1 tsp baking powder
50 g / 1 ¾ oz / ½ cup ground almonds
150 g / 5 oz / ⅔ cup caster (superfine) sugar
150 g / 5 oz / ⅔ cup butter, softened
3 large eggs
2 tbsp unsweetened cocoa powder

HOT CHOCOLATE SAUCE
175 ml / 6 fl. oz / ⅔ cup milk
2 tbsp double (heavy) cream
2 tbsp caster (superfine) sugar
200 g / 7 oz dark chocolate, melted

- Preheat the oven to 180°C (160°C fan) / 350F / gas 4 and grease and line a loaf tin with greaseproof paper.
- Sieve the flour and baking powder into a mixing bowl then add the ground almonds, sugar, butter and eggs and whisk with an electric whisk for 4 minutes or until pale and well whipped.
- Divide the mixture into 2 bowls. Mix the cocoa powder with 2 tablespoons of hot water until smooth and stir it into one of the bowls.
- Spoon the mixtures into the tin, alternating between chocolate and plain, then draw a knife through the middle to marble.
- Bake for 45–50 minutes. The cake is ready when a toothpick inserted comes out clean.
- For the sauce, bring the milk, cream and sugar to the boil in a saucepan over a medium heat, whisking continuously. Pour over the melted chocolate and whisk until well combined.
- Transfer the cake to a wire rack to cool completely before slicing. Drizzle over the hot chocolate sauce, to serve.

Raisin and chocolate brioche

PREPARATION TIME: 1 hour, 15 minutes
COOKING TIME: 30 minutes
SERVES: 8

125 ml / 4 ⅓ fl. oz / ½ cup milk
1 egg
160 g / 5 ⅔ oz / 1 cup plain (all-purpose) flour
160 g / 5 ⅔ oz / 1 cup strong white bread flour
1 tsp salt
1 ½ tbsp sugar
½ tbsp easy-blend dried yeast
200 g / 7 oz / ¾ cup unsalted butter, chilled and cubed
100 g / 3 ½ oz / ½ cup raisins
100 g / 3 ½ oz / ⅔ cup chocolate chips

- Lightly grease a 23 cm x 13 cm (9 in x 5 in) loaf tin. Warm the milk with 3 tbsp water, add the egg and whisk.

- Place the flours, salt, sugar and yeast in a food processor and mix, then add the butter a little at a time and pulse to cut the butter into the flour. Don't let it become breadcrumbs.

- Tip the flour-butter mixture into a bowl, make a well in the middle and add the milk mixture, raisins and chocolate chips, then fold together with a fork. It does not need to be completely smooth.

- Pour into the loaf tin, cover with cling film and leave to prove in a warm draught-free place for 1 hour. Preheat the oven to 200°C (180°C fan) / 400F / gas 6.

- Remove the cling film and bake for about 30 minutes or until risen and golden. Leave to cool before eating.

Chocolate and cranberry brioche
Replace the raisins for equal amounts of dried cranberries for a delicious sour and sweet taste.

Wholemeal fruit cake

PREPARATION TIME: 15 minutes
COOKING TIME: 55 minutes
SERVES: 8

200 g / 7 oz / 1 ⅓ cups self-raising flour
200 g / 7 oz / 1 ⅓ cups wholemeal flour
100 g / 3 ½ oz / ½ cup butter, cubed
100 g / 3 ½ oz / ½ cup caster (superfine) sugar
1 large egg
75 ml / 2 ⅔ fl. oz / ⅓ cup milk
75 g / 2 ⅔ oz / ⅓ cup raisins
75 g / 2 ⅔ oz / ½ cup glacé cherries, chopped

- Preheat the oven to 180°C (160°C fan) / 350F / gas 4 and line a loaf tin with non-stick baking paper.
- Sieve both flours into a mixing bowl and rub in the butter until it resembles fine breadcrumbs then stir in the sugar.
- Lightly beat the egg with the milk and stir it into the dry ingredients with the fruit until just combined then scrape the mixture into the tin.
- Bake the cake for 55 minutes or until a skewer inserted comes out clean.
- Transfer the cake to a wire rack and leave to cool.

Lemon custard tart

PREPARATION TIME: 40 minutes
COOKING TIME: 45 minutes
SERVES: 8

100 g / 3 ½ oz / ½ cup butter, cubed
200 g / 7 oz / 1 ⅓ cups plain (all-purpose) flour
2 large egg yolks
75 ml / 2 ⅔ fl. oz / ¼ cup runny honey
1 tsp cornflour (cornstarch)
225 ml / 8 fl. oz / ¾ cup milk
2 lemons, juiced and zested

- Preheat the oven to 200°C (180°C fan) / 400F / gas 6.
- Rub the butter into the flour and add just enough cold water to bind.
- Chill for 30 minutes then roll out on a floured surface. Use the pastry to line a 23 cm (9 in) round tart case.
- Prick the pastry with a fork, line with oven-safe cling film and fill with baking beans.
- Bake for 10 minutes then remove the cling film and baking beans. Cook for a further 8 minutes to crisp.
- Reduce the oven temperature to 160°C (140°C fan) / 325F / gas 3.
- Whisk together the egg yolks, honey, cornflour, milk, lemon juice and zest and pour it into the pastry case.
- Bake for 25 minutes or until the filling is just set in the middle.
- Leave to cool before slicing.

Gingerbread heart biscuits

PREPARATION TIME: 20 minutes
COOKING TIME: 12–15 minutes
MAKES: 20

175 g / 6 oz / 1 ¼ cups plain (all-purpose) flour
1 tsp mixed spice
1 tsp ground ginger
75 g / 2 ⅔ oz / ⅓ cup caster (superfine) sugar
150 g / 5 oz / ⅔ cup butter, cubed

FOR THE FONDANT ICING
500 g / 17 ⅔ oz ready-to-roll fondant icing (in red, pink and white)
icing pen (white and red)

- Preheat the oven to 180°C (160°C fan) / 350F / gas 4 and line a baking tray with greaseproof paper.
- Mix together the flour, mixed spice, ginger and caster sugar in a bowl, then rub in the butter.
- Knead gently until the mixture forms a smooth dough then roll out on a lightly floured surface to 6 mm (¼ in) thick.
- Use a heart-shaped cookie cutter to cut out the biscuits and spread them out on the baking tray.
- Bake the biscuits for 12–15 minutes, turning the tray round halfway through.
- Transfer the biscuits to a wire rack and leave to cool.
- For the fondant icing, roll out the fondant for each colour (red, pink and white) and use the same heart-shaped cutter to cut out heart fondant shapes for each biscuit.
- Gently press the fondant shapes on each biscuit and decorate your chosen pattern using the icing pen.

Chocolate hazelnut spread

PREPARATION TIME: **5 minutes**
COOKING TIME: **45 minutes**
MAKES: **400g / 14 oz**

50 g / 1 ¾ oz / ½ cup hazelnuts (cob nuts)

100 g / 3 ½ oz / ½ cup golden caster sugar

200 ml / 7 fl. oz / ¾ cup double (heavy) cream

200 g / 7 oz dark chocolate, minimum 60% cocoa solids, chopped

pinch of sea salt

- Set an oven to 200°C (180°C fan) / 400F / gas 6. Spread the hazelnuts on a baking tray and place in the oven for 10 minutes or until golden. Then leave to cool completely.
- Place the hazelnuts in a food processor and blend with the caster sugar until smooth.
- Heat the cream until it starts to simmer, then pour in the chopped chocolate and stir until the mixture has thickened.
- Add the hazelnut paste and fold carefully adding a pinch of salt.
- Leave to cool to room temperature for a spreadable consistency.

Grilled pineapple with honey

PREPARATION TIME: **5 minutes**
COOKING TIME: **10–15 minutes**
SERVES: **6–8**

150 ml / 5 ⅓ fl. oz / ⅔ cup pineapple juice

1 lime, juiced and zest thinly pared

12 pineapple rings

3 tbsp runny honey

3–4 fresh mint leaves, to serve

2–3 rosemary sprigs, to serve

- Put the pineapple juice, lime juice and pineapple rings in a saucepan and bring to a gentle simmer.
- Stew the pineapple for 10 minutes, then leave to cool completely.
- Drizzle the pineapple with runny honey and serve with some fresh mint leaves and rosemary sprigs.

Grilled pineapple with zesty maple
For a zesty alternative, replace the honey with maple and lemon syrup. Simply mix 3 tablespoons of maple syrup with the zest and juice of a lemon.

THE COOKERY COLLECTION

Chocolate cinnamon buns

PREPARATION TIME: 3 hours, 30 minutes
COOKING TIME: 35 minutes
MAKES: 12

400 g / 14 oz / 2 ⅔ cups strong white bread flour
½ tsp easy-blend dried yeast
4 tbsp caster (superfine) sugar
1 tsp fine sea salt
1 tbsp ground cinnamon
1 tbsp olive oil
280 ml / 9 ¾ fl. oz / 1 cup warm water
75 g / 2 ⅔ oz / ½ cup dark brown sugar
2 tbsp butter, softened
50 g / 1 ¾ oz / ⅓ cup chocolate chips
1 egg, beaten

- Combine flour, yeast, caster sugar, salt and cinnamon. Stir the oil into the water then stir into the dry ingredients.
- Knead the dough on an oiled surface until smooth.
- Leave the dough to rest in a lightly oiled bowl, covered with cling film, for 1–2 hours.
- Knead the dough for 2 minutes, then roll into a rectangle.
- Cream the brown sugar and butter together and stir in the chocolate chips.
- Spread the mixture over the dough and roll it up tightly.
- Cut into 12 slices and arrange in a round cake tin.
- Cover the rolls with oiled cling film and leave to prove for 1 hour or until doubled in size.
- Preheat the oven to 220°C (200°C fan) / 425F / gas 7.
- Brush the rolls with egg then transfer the tray to the top shelf of the oven and bake for 35 minutes.
- Leave to cool before breaking into individual rolls.

Carrot and pecan cake

PREPARATION TIME: 20 minutes
COOKING TIME: 40–45 minutes
SERVES: 8–10

175 g / 6 oz / 1 cup soft light brown sugar

2 large eggs

150 ml / 5 ⅓ fl. oz / ⅔ cup coconut oil

175 g / 6 oz / 1 ¼ cups stone-ground wholemeal flour

3 tsp baking powder

2 tsp ground cinnamon

1 orange, zest finely grated

200 g / 7 oz / 1 ⅔ cups carrots, washed and coarsely grated

100 g / 3 ½ oz / ¾ cup pecans, chopped, plus extra for decorating

FOR THE ICING

110 g / 4 oz / ½ cup cream cheese

55 g / 2 oz / ¼ cup butter, softened

110 g / 4 oz / 1 cup icing (confectioners') sugar

1 tsp vanilla extract

- Preheat the oven to 190°C (170°C fan) / 375F / gas 5 and line a 23 cm (9 in) square cake tin with greaseproof paper.
- Whisk the sugar, eggs and oil together for 3 minutes.
- Fold in the flour, baking powder and cinnamon, followed by the orange zest, carrots and pecans.
- Scrape into a loaf tin and bake for 40–45 minutes.
- Test with a wooden toothpick, if it comes out clean, the cake is done.
- Transfer the cake to a wire rack and leave to cool.
- To make the icing, beat the cream cheese and butter together with a wooden spoon until light and fluffy then beat in the icing sugar a little at a time.
- Add the vanilla extract then use a whisk to whip the mixture for 1–2 minutes, until smooth and light.
- Spread the icing over the cake and sprinkle with some more chopped pecans.

Carrot and raisin cake
Add 100 g / 3 ½ oz / ½ cup raisins to the wet ingredients before adding the cake mixture to the loaf tin and baking.

Iced lemon drizzle cake

PREPARATION TIME: **10 minutes**
COOKING TIME: **35–40 minutes**
SERVES: **8**

175 g / 6 oz / 1 ¼ cups self-raising flour, sifted
1 tsp baking powder
175 g / 6 oz / ¾ cup caster (superfine) sugar
175 g / 6 oz / ¾ cup butter, softened
3 large eggs
2 lemons, zest finely grated

FOR THE ICING
2 tbsp lemon juice
½ tsp vanilla extract
3 tbsp caster (superfine) sugar
3 tbsp icing (confectioners') sugar

- Preheat the oven to 180°C (160°C fan) / 350F / gas 4 and oil and line a 23 cm (9 in) round cake tin with greaseproof paper.
- Combine the flour, baking powder, sugar, butter, eggs and lemon zest in a bowl and whisk together for 2 minutes or until smooth.
- Scrape the mixture into the tin and level the top then bake for 35–40 minutes or until a toothpick inserted comes out clean.
- Mix the lemon juice with the vanilla extract, caster sugar and icing sugar and drizzle it all over the cake when it comes out of the oven.
- Leave the cake to cool in its tin for 20 minutes then transfer it to a wire rack and leave to cool completely.

Hazelnut and raisin bread

PREPARATION TIME: 2 hours
COOKING TIME: 25 minutes
MAKES: 1 loaf

475 g / 16 ¾ oz / 3 ¼ cups malthouse flour
1 tbsp soft brown sugar
1 ½ tsp salt
1 ½ tsp fast-action dried yeast
2 tbsp vegetable oil
325 ml / 11 fl. oz / 1 ⅓ cups warm water
200 g / 7 oz / 1 ⅔ cups hazelnuts (cob nuts), chopped
75 g / 2 ⅔ oz / ⅓ cup raisins
chocolate spread, to serve (optional)

- Mix the flour, sugar, salt and yeast in a bowl, add the oil and stir in enough water to make a smooth dough.
- Knead on a floured surface for 5 minutes until smooth and elastic. Work in the hazelnuts and raisins, then return to the bowl. Cover loosely and leave in a warm place to rise for 1 hour or until doubled in size.
- Tip onto a floured surface, knead well for 5 minutes then shape into an oval loaf.
- Transfer to a greased baking sheet and make deep slashes in the top. Cover loosely and leave to rise for 30 minutes or until twice as big again.
- Preheat the oven to 200°C (180°C fan) / 400F / gas 6.
- Sprinkle with a little extra flour, lightly spray with water and bake for 25 minutes or until browned and the bread sounds hollow when tapped.
- Transfer to a wire rack to cool. Serve with some chocolate spread.

Chocolate chip and hazelnut bread
Replace the raisins with the same quantity of chocolate chips for a truly decadent loaf.

Chocolate jam cake

PREPARATION TIME: **20 minutes**
COOKING TIME: **25 minutes**
SERVES: **8**

100 g / 3 ½ oz / ⅔ cup self-raising flour
1 tsp baking powder
100 g / 3 ½ oz / ½ cup caster (superfine) sugar
100 g / 3 ½ oz / ½ cup butter, softened
2 large eggs
450 g / 1 lb / 1 ¾ cups raspberry jam (jelly)

TOPPING
100 g / 3 ½ oz milk chocolate, melted
a handful of walnuts, chopped
a handful of redcurrants

- Preheat the oven to 180°C (160°C fan) / 350F /
  gas 4 and butter a 20 cm / 8 in square cake tin.
- Sieve the flour and baking powder into a
  mixing bowl and add sugar, butter and eggs.
- Beat the mixture with an electric whisk for
  4 minutes or until smooth and well whipped.
- Spread the raspberry jam in the cake tin and
  spoon the cake mixture on top.
- Level the top with a palette knife and bake for
  25 minutes or until a skewer inserted comes
  out clean.
- Leave the cake to cool for 10 minutes before
  turning out onto a plate, jam-side up.
- To decorate, simply drizzle the milk chocolate
  over the jam and evenly distribute the
  redcurrants. Scatter some chopped walnuts
  over the top, then serve.

Zesty fig muffins

PREPARATION TIME: **15 minutes**
COOKING TIME: **20–25 minutes**
MAKES: **12**

1 large egg
120 ml / 4 ¼ fl. oz / ½ cup olive oil
120 ml / 4 ¼ fl. oz / ½ cup milk
375 g / 13 oz / 2 ½ cups self-raising flour, sifted
1 tsp baking powder
200 g / 7 oz / ¾ cup caster (superfine) sugar
1 orange, zest finely grated
4 dried figs, chopped
4 fresh figs, sliced, to garnish
icing (confectioners') sugar, to garnish

- Preheat the oven to 180°C (160°C fan) / 350F / gas 4 and line a 12-hole muffin tin with muffin cases.
- Beat the egg in a jug with the oil and milk until well mixed.
- Mix the flour, baking powder, sugar and orange zest in a bowl. Pour in the egg mixture and stir just enough to combine, then fold through the dried figs.
- Divide the mixture between the muffin cases and bake for 20–25 minutes. Test with a wooden toothpick, if it comes out clean, the cakes are done.
- Transfer the muffins to a wire rack and leave to cool completely. Garnish each muffin with a slice of fresh fig and sprinkle generously with icing sugar.

Fig and lemon muffins
Replace the orange zest with the same amount of lemon zest and add the juice of 1 lemon to the wet ingredients before baking.

Rich chocolate torte

PREPARATION TIME: **40 minutes**
COOKING TIME: **55 minutes**
SERVES: **8**

100 g / 3 ½ oz / ½ cup butter, cubed
200 g / 7 oz / 1 ⅓ cups plain (all-purpose) flour
4 large egg yolks
75 g / 2 ⅔ oz / ⅓ cup caster (superfine) sugar
½ tsp vanilla powder
2 tsp cornflour (cornstarch)
2 tbsp unsweetened cocoa powder
450 ml / 16 fl. oz / 1 ¾ cups milk

- Preheat the oven to 200°C (180°C fan) / 400F / gas 6.
- Rub the butter into the flour and add cold water to bind. Chill for 30 minutes then roll out on a floured surface. Use the pastry to line a 23 cm (9 in) round tart case.
- Prick the pastry with a fork, line with oven-safe cling film and fill with baking beans.
- Bake for 10 minutes then remove the cling film and baking beans and cook for a further 8 minutes to crisp.
- Reduce the oven temperature to 160°C (140°C fan) / 325F / gas 3.
- Whisk together the egg yolks, sugar, vanilla powder, cornflour, cocoa and milk and strain it through a sieve into the pastry case.
- Bake the tart for 35 minutes. Leave to cool, then serve.

Rich chocolate orange torte
Add the zest of 1 orange and a few drops of natural orange essence to the wet ingredients before baking.

Zesty hot cross buns

PREPARATION TIME: 3 hours, 15 minutes
COOKING TIME: 15–20 minutes
MAKES: 16

55 g / 2 oz / ¼ cup butter, cubed

400 g / 14 oz / 2 ⅔ cups strong white bread flour, plus extra for dusting

½ tsp easy-blend dried yeast

4 tbsp caster (superfine) sugar

1 tsp fine sea salt

2 tsp ground ginger

100 g / 3 ½ oz orange peel, finely chopped

50 g / 1 ¾ oz / ¼ cup sultanas

80 ml / 3 fl. oz / ⅓ cup orange juice

200 ml / 6 ¾ fl. oz / ¾ cup warm water

4 tbsp plain (all-purpose) flour

1 egg, beaten

marmalade, for spreading

- Rub the butter into the bread flour and stir in the yeast, sugar, salt and ground ginger. Mix the orange peel and sultanas with the orange juice and warm water, then stir it into the dry ingredients.
- Knead the mixture on a lightly oiled surface for 10 minutes or until the dough is smooth and elastic.
- Leave the dough to rest, covered with the mixing bowl, for 1–2 hours, until doubled in size.
- Shape the dough into 12 buns and transfer to a greased baking tray, then cover and leave to prove for 45 minutes.
- Preheat the oven to 220°C (200°C fan) / 425F / gas 7.
- Mix the plain flour with just enough water to make a thick paste. Spoon the paste into a piping bag.
- Brush the buns with egg and pipe a cross on top of each one.
- Bake for 15–20 minutes or until golden brown and cooked through.
- Leave to cool on a wire rack then split in half. Spread thickly with some marmalade and serve.

Lemon hot cross buns
For something a little different, swap the orange peel for the zest of 2 lemons and replace the orange juice with fresh lemon juice. Serve with some lemon curd.

Cranberry and redcurrant topless cake

PREPARATION TIME: **10 minutes**
COOKING TIME: **30 minutes**
SERVES: **6**

110 g / 4 oz / ⅔ cup self-raising flour, sifted
110 g / 4 oz / ½ cup caster (superfine) sugar
110 g / 4 oz / ½ cup butter, softened
2 large eggs
125 g / 4 ⅓ oz / ½ cup redcurrant jelly
300 g / 10 ½ oz / 2 cups stewed cranberries
fresh mint leaves, to garnish
icing (confectioners') sugar, to dust

- Preheat the oven to 190°C (170°C fan) / 375F / gas 5 and butter a baking dish.
- Combine the flour, sugar, butter and eggs in a bowl and whisk together for 2 minutes or until smooth.
- Spoon the cake mixture into the baking dish and transfer to the oven. Bake for 30 minutes.
- Test with a wooden toothpick, if it comes out clean, the cake is done.
- Scoop out the top layer of the cake and leave 2 cm (1 in) of cake from the outside rim.
- Spread the redcurrant jelly over the top and spoon the stewed cranberries on top.
- Arrange the fresh mint leaves on top of the pudding. Dust the top with icing sugar before serving.

Lemon fruit cake

PREPARATION TIME: **15 minutes**
COOKING TIME: **55 minutes**
SERVES: **8**

225 g / 8 oz / 1 ½ cups self-raising flour
100 g / 3 ½ oz / ½ cup butter, cubed
100 g / 3 ½ oz / ½ cup caster (superfine) sugar
1 large egg
50 ml / 1 ¾ fl. oz / ¼ cup milk
2 lemons, juiced and zested
75 g / 2 ⅔ oz / ⅓ cup sultanas
icing (confectioners') sugar, to decorate
edible flowers, to decorate (optional)

- Preheat the oven to 180°C (160°C fan) / 350F / gas 4 and line a 23 cm (9 in) round cake tin with greaseproof paper.
- Sieve the flour into a mixing bowl and rub in the butter until it resembles fine breadcrumbs then stir in the sugar.
- Lightly beat the egg with the milk, lemon juice and zest. Stir it into the dry ingredients and add the sultanas and mix until just combined, then scrape the mixture into the tin.
- Bake for 55 minutes or until a skewer inserted comes out clean.
- Transfer the cake to a wire rack. Leave to cool then top with some icing sugar and a few edible flowers.

Almond croissants

PREPARATION TIME: 4 hours
COOKING TIME: 30 minutes
MAKES: 8

350 g / 12 oz / 2 ⅓ cups strong white bread flour
1 tsp easy-blend yeast
75 ml / 2 ⅔ fl. oz / ⅓ cup warm water
2 large eggs, separated
75 ml / 2 ⅔ fl. oz / ⅓ cup milk
50 ml / 1 ¾ fl. oz / ¼ cup double (heavy) cream
2 tbsp caster (superfine) sugar, plus extra for
dusting
1 tsp salt
250 g / 9 oz / 1 ¼ cups butter, chilled and cubed
a handful of flaked (slivered) almonds

- Mix 50 g / 1 ¾ oz / ⅓ cup of the flour with the
  yeast and warm water, and leave somewhere
  warm for 1 hour.
- Whisk the egg yolks with the milk, cream,
  sugar and salt, then slowly incorporate it into
  the yeast mixture.
- Mix in the butter cubes and remaining flour,
  then knead briefly on a floured surface.
- Roll out the dough, then fold into thirds and
  roll again. Fold it into thirds then chill for
  30 minutes.
- Repeat the rolling, folding and chilling
  twice more.
- Roll the dough into a square, cut into
  quarters and cut each one diagonally into
  2 triangles. Roll into croissant shapes, then
  transfer them to a lined baking tray. Cover
  the croissants with cling film and leave to rise
  for 1 hour.
- Preheat the oven to 200°C (180°C fan) / 400F
  / gas 6.
- Sprinkle the almonds on top. Brush the
  croissants with egg white and bake for
  30 minutes, reducing the heat to 180°C
  (160°C fan) / 350F / gas 4 after the first
  10 minutes.
- Remove from the oven once the croissants
  have risen and are golden on top. Sieve some
  icing sugar on top before serving.

Desserts

Chocolate and apple crumble pots

PREPARATION TIME: **5 minutes**
COOKING TIME: **20 minutes**
SERVES: **6**

4 large cooking apples, peeled and diced
2 tbsp caster (superfine) sugar
6 digestive biscuits, crushed
100 g / 3 ½ oz / ⅔ cup milk chocolate chips

- Preheat the oven to 220°C (200°C fan) / 425F / gas 7.
- Put the apples and sugar in a saucepan with 3 tablespoons of cold water.
- Put a lid on the pan then cook over a gentle heat for 10 minutes, stirring occasionally.
- Take the pan off the heat and mash the apples with the back of a fork or potato masher.
- Divide the mixture between 6 ovenproof glass ramekins and sprinkle with the crushed biscuits and chocolate chips.
- Bake the crumbles for 5–7 minutes until the top of each crumble is nicely toasted.

Chocolate and pear crumble pots
Replace the apple with the same amount of peeled and diced pear. Conference pears are the best variety for this recipe.

Vanilla crème brûlée

PREPARATION TIME: **5 minutes**
COOKING TIME: **10–15 minutes**
CHILLING TIME: **25 minutes**
SERVES: **6**

450 ml / 16 fl. oz / 1 ¾ cups whole milk
4 large egg yolks
75 g / 2 ⅔ oz / ⅓ cup caster (superfine) sugar, plus extra for sprinkling
2 tsp cornflour (cornstarch)
1 tsp vanilla extract
3 tbsp granulated sugar
3 vanilla pods, halved

- Pour the milk into a saucepan and bring to simmering point. Meanwhile, whisk the egg yolks with the caster sugar, cornflour and vanilla extract until thick.
- Gradually incorporate the hot milk, whisking all the time, then scrape the mixture back into the saucepan.
- Stir the custard over a low heat until it thickens.
- Pour the custard into 6 individual ramekins and chill in the fridge for 25 minutes.
- Sprinkle the tops with sugar then caramelize with a blowtorch, or under a hot grill.
- Garnish with half a vanilla pod, then serve.

THE COOKERY COLLECTION

Lemon cream tarts

PREPARATION TIME: 40 minutes
COOKING TIME: 25–30 minutes
MAKES: 6

3 lemons, juiced
175 g / 6 oz / ¾ cup caster (superfine) sugar
2 tsp cornflour (cornstarch)
4 large eggs, beaten
225 ml / 8 fl. oz / ¾ cup double (heavy) cream
clotted cream, to serve (optional)
fresh mint leaves, to garnish

FOR THE PASTRY
150 g / 5 oz / ⅔ cup butter, cubed and chilled
300 g / 10 ½ oz / 2 cups plain (all-purpose) flour

- To make the pastry, rub the butter into the flour until the mixture resembles fine breadcrumbs. Stir in just enough cold water to bring the pastry together into a dough.
- Leave the pastry to chill in the fridge for 30 minutes.
- Preheat the oven to 200°C (180°C fan) / 400F / gas 6.
- Roll out the pastry on a floured surface and use it to line 6 individual tart cases. Line them with oven-safe cling film and fill with baking beans then blind bake for 10 minutes.
- Remove the pastry cases from the oven and reduce the heat to 160°C (140°C fan) / 325F / gas 3.
- Stir the lemon juice into the caster sugar and cornflour to dissolve, then whisk in the eggs and cream.
- Strain the mixture into the pastry cases and bake for 15–20 minutes or until just set in the middle.
- Serve the tarts with a dollop of clotted cream and some mint leaves.

Lemon and lime tarts
Combine the juice of 2 limes and 1 lemon with the caster sugar and cornflour (cornstarch) before whisking in the eggs and cream.

Chai rice pudding

PREPARATION TIME: **25 minutes**
COOKING TIME: **1 hour, 30 minutes**
SERVES: **4**

1.2 litres / 2 pints 4 fl. oz / 4 ¾ cups coconut milk
2 star anise
4 cardamom pods
6 cloves
50 g / 1 ¾ oz coconut oil
110 g / 4 oz / ½ cup short grain rice
75 g / 2 ⅔ oz / ⅓ cup caster (superfine) sugar
4 tbsp maple syrup
4 cinnamon sticks, to garnish
1 tsp ground cinnamon, to garnish (optional)
4 star anise, to garnish (optional)

- Preheat the oven to 140°C (120°C fan) / 275F / gas 1.
- Warm the milk in a saucepan with the spices then leave to infuse for 20 minutes.
- Melt the oil in a cast-iron casserole dish and add the rice and sugar.
- Stir over a low heat for 2 minutes then gradually incorporate the hot milk and spices.
- Cover the dish and bake in the oven for 1 hour 30 minutes, then spoon into 4 bowls.
- Drizzle over the maple syrup and sprinkle some ground cinnamon on top. Garnish with a cinnamon stick and a whole star anise (optional).

Spiced vanilla almond rice pudding
Add half a teaspoon of ground vanilla to the spiced milk and sprinkle with some toasted flaked (slivered) almonds for a nutty variation.

Chocolate and pear tart

PREPARATION TIME: **40 minutes**
COOKING TIME: **30–35 minutes**
SERVES: **8**

110 g / 4 oz / ½ cup butter, cubed and chilled
225 g / 8 oz / 1 ½ cups plain (all-purpose) flour
200 g / 7 oz dark chocolate (min. 60% cocoa solids), chopped
4 pears, cored and sliced
100 g / 3 ½ oz dark chocolate (min. 60% cocoa solids), melted

Chocolate, coconut and pear tart
Sprinkle 2 tablespoons of desiccated coconut on
the tart with the drizzled chocolate before serving.

- Rub the butter into the flour then add just enough cold water to bind the mixture into a dough.
- Roll out the pastry on a floured surface and use it to line a 23 cm (9 in) round tart case.
- Leave the pastry to chill in the fridge for 30 minutes.
- Preheat the oven to 200°C (180°C fan) / 400F / gas 6.
- Line the pastry case with oven-safe cling film and fill it with baking beans, then blind bake for 15 minutes.
- Remove the cling film and baking beans and fill the case with chopped chocolate then arrange the pear slices on top.
- Bake for 15–20 minutes or until the pears are soft and golden.
- Drizzle the tart with the melted dark chocolate to create a decorative pattern just before serving.

Blueberry and mint cheesecake

PREPARATION TIME: 20 minutes
COOKING TIME: 40–50 minutes
CHILLING TIME: 2 hours
SERVES: 10–12

200 g / 7 oz digestive biscuits, crushed
50 g / 1 ¾ oz / ¼ cup butter, melted
600 g / 1 lb 5 oz / 2 ½ cups cream cheese
150 ml / 5 ⅓ fl. oz / ⅔ cup soured cream
175 g / 6 oz / ¾ cup caster (superfine) sugar
2 large eggs, plus 1 egg yolk
2 tbsp plain (all-purpose) flour
1 tsp mint extract
100 g / 3 ½ oz / ⅔ cup blueberries

FOR THE BLUEBERRY TOPPING
100 g / 3 ½ oz / ½ cup blueberry jam (jelly)
200 g / 7 oz / 1 ⅓ cups blueberries
fresh mint leaves, to garnish

- Preheat the oven to 180°C (160°C fan) / 350F / gas 4 and grease a 20 cm (8 in) round spring-form cake tin.
- Mix the crushed biscuits with the butter and press into an even layer in the bottom of the tin.
- Bake the biscuit layer for 5 minutes or until firm.
- Whisk together the remaining cheesecake ingredients until smooth.
- Spoon the cheesecake mixture on top of the biscuit base and bake for 40–50 minutes or until the middle is only just set.
- Leave to cool completely in the tin.
- To make the topping, heat the jam in a small pan until it turns runny then stir in the blueberries. Spoon this mixture on top of the cheesecake.
- Transfer the tin to the fridge and chill for 2 hours before unmoulding and cutting into slices.
- Garnish with some fresh mint leaves.

Blueberry and vanilla cheesecake
Replace the mint extract with the same amount of vanilla essence and garnish with a fresh vanilla pod.

Key lime pie

PREPARATION TIME: 10 minutes
COOKING TIME: 25–30 minutes
SERVES: 10

2 tsp cornflour (cornstarch)
8 limes, juiced and zest finely grated
4 large eggs, beaten
225 g / 8 oz / 1 cup butter
175 g / 6 oz / ¾ cup caster (superfine) sugar

FOR THE BASE
200 g / 7 oz ginger biscuits, crushed
3 tbsp butter, melted
2 tbsp ground ginger

FOR THE MERINGUE
4 large eggs, separated, whites
100 g / 3 ½ oz / ½ cup caster (superfine) sugar
½ lime, zested to garnish

- Preheat the oven to 200°C (180°C fan) / 400F / gas 6.
- For the base, mix the crushed biscuits with the butter and ground ginger. Press into an even layer in the bottom of a 23 cm (9 in) round tart case.
- Bake the biscuit layer for 5 minutes or until firm.
- Meanwhile, dissolve the cornflour in the lime juice and put it in a saucepan with the rest of the main ingredients.
- Stir constantly over a medium heat to melt the butter and dissolve the sugar. Bring to a gentle simmer then pour it onto the biscuit base.
- For the meringue, whisk the egg whites until stiff, then gradually add the sugar and whisk until the mixture is thick and shiny.
- Spoon the meringue on top of the lime curd, then bake for 10 minutes or until golden brown on top.
- Cut the pie into slices and garnish with some lime zest.

Lemon meringue pie
For a zingy lemon alternative, replace the limes with 8 lemons, juiced and zest finely grated, and follow the same method. To garnish, sprinkle over the zest of half a lemon.

Toffee and almond pavlova

PREPARATION TIME: 30 minutes
COOKING TIME: 1 hour
SERVES: 6

225 ml / 8 fl. oz / ¾ cup double (heavy) cream
2 tbsp icing (confectioners') sugar
½ tsp vanilla extract
toffee sauce, to drizzle
100 g / 3 ½ oz / 1 ⅓ cups flaked (slivered) almonds, toasted

FOR THE ALMOND MERINGUE
4 large egg, separated, whites
110 g / 4 oz / ½ cup caster (superfine) sugar
1 tsp cornflour (cornstarch)
55 g / 2 oz / ½ cup ground almonds

Three-tiered meringue
For a three-tiered meringue, repeat the method twice more to make three separate layers.

- Preheat the oven to 140°C (120°C fan) / 275F / gas 1 and oil and line a medium-sized round cake tin with greaseproof paper.
- To make the meringue, whisk the egg whites until stiff, then gradually whisk in half the sugar until the mixture is very shiny.
- Fold in the remaining sugar with the cornflour and ground almonds then spoon the mixture into the medium-sized round cake tin.
- Bake the meringue for 1 hour or until crisp on the outside, but still a bit chewy in the middle. Leave to cool completely, then transfer the meringue to a serving plate.
- Whip the cream with the icing sugar and vanilla until it just holds its shape, then spoon it into a piping bag fitted with a large star nozzle, and pipe an even layer on top of the meringue.
- Drizzle with some of the toffee sauce and sprinkle the flaked almonds on top for extra indulgence.

Blueberry pie

PREPARATION TIME: **1 hour**
COOKING TIME: **25–30 minutes**
SERVES: **12**

200 g / 7 oz / ¾ cup butter, cubed and chilled
400 g / 14 oz / 2 ⅔ cups plain (all-purpose) flour
400 g / 14 oz / 2 ⅔ cups blueberries
4 tbsp caster (superfine) sugar
½ tsp cornflour (cornstarch)
1 egg, beaten

- Rub the butter into the flour then stir in just enough cold water to make the pastry into a dough.
- Wrap the dough in cling film and chill for 30 minutes.
- Preheat the oven to 200°C (180°C fan) / 400F / gas 6.
- Roll out half the pastry on a floured surface and cut out a large circle to line a medium-sized round baking tin.
- Toss the blueberries with the sugar and cornflour and place the filling on top of the pastry in the tin. Make sure the mixture is evenly spread.
- Roll out the rest of the pastry into a square shape and cut into 9 individual strips about 1 cm (½ in) wide.
- Carefully place the first 5 strips across the pie vertically and the remaining 4 over the top horizontally, forming a lattice pattern. Brush the strips with egg and press down firmly round the outside.
- Bake in the oven for 25–30 minutes. Transfer the pie to a wire rack to cool.

Blueberry pie with coconut cream
Serve the pie with some delicious home-made coconut cream. Simply blend 400 ml / 14 fl. oz / 1 ⅔ cup coconut milk with 1 teaspoon of vanilla extract and 2 tablespoons of sugar, then serve on the side.

Bread and butter berry pudding

PREPARATION TIME: **40 minutes**
COOKING TIME: **40 minutes**
SERVES: **12**

1 loaf white bread, cut into thick slices
3 tbsp butter, softened
200 g / 7 oz / ¾ cup strawberry jam (jelly)
250 ml / 9 fl. oz / 1 cup whole milk
200 ml / 6 ¾ fl. oz / ¾ cup double (heavy) cream
4 large egg yolks
75 g / 2 ⅔ oz / ⅓ cup caster (superfine) sugar
a handful of blackcurrants
a handful of strawberries, sliced

- Spread the bread with butter and cut into triangles.
- Arrange the triangles in a baking dish, spreading thin layers of the jam as you go.
- Whisk the milk, cream, eggs and caster sugar together and pour it over the top, then leave to soak for 30 minutes.
- Preheat the oven to 180°C (160°C fan) / 350F / gas 4.
- Add the blackcurrants and strawberries on top of the pudding, ensuring they are spread evenly.
- Bake the pudding for 40 minutes or until the top is golden brown.

Bread and butter plum pudding
Replace the strawberry jam (jelly) with the same amount of plum jam (jelly) and swap the berries for plums. Wash and remove the stones from 6 ripe plums. Roughly chop and spread on top of the pudding before baking.

Chilled lime and cashew cheesecake

PREPARATION TIME: overnight
CHILLING TIME: overnight
SERVES: 10–12

FOR THE BASE
50 g / 1 ¾ oz / ½ cup almonds
4 dates, stones removed
1 tsp coconut oil, melted
pinch Himalayan salt

FOR THE CASHEW CREAM
100 g / 3 ½ oz / ¾ cup cashew nuts, soaked in water overnight
2 tbsp agave nectar
1 ½ limes, juiced
3 tsp coconut oil, melted
75 ml / 2 ⅔ fl. oz / ⅓ cup coconut cream
pinch Himalayan salt
1 lime, zested

FOR THE LIME TOPPING
½ lime, sliced
2 limes, zested

- To make the base, add the almonds to a food processor and pulse until they are roughly chopped. Then add the remaining base ingredients and pulse until a sticky paste forms.
- Line a medium-sized round cake tin with baking paper and grease with a little coconut oil.
- Add the base mixture to the bottom of the tin and press down firmly until the base is evenly spread. Place in the fridge.
- To make the cashew cream, add the soaked cashew nuts, agave, lime juice and coconut oil. Blend until fully incorporated and slowly add the coconut cream until the mixture is smooth. Add the salt and lime zest and blend.
- Spoon the cashew cream mixture on top of the base and leave in the fridge overnight to set.
- To make the topping, add the lime slices and sprinkle some lime zest over the top. Serve cold.

Chilled lemon and lime cheesecake
Add the juice and zest of 2 lemons to the cashew cream for a citrus kick.

Stewed cherries with coconut yogurt

PREPARATION TIME: 10 minutes
COOKING TIME: 15 minutes
SERVES: 4

100 ml / 3 ½ fl. oz / ½ cup rose wine
100 g / 3 ½ oz / ½ cup caster (superfine) sugar
450 g / 1 lb / 3 cups cherries, stoned
3 tbsp kirsch
1 tsp almond essence
450 g / 1 lb / 1 ¾ cups coconut yogurt
75 g / 2 ⅔ oz / ¾ cup icing (confectioners') sugar
1 biscotti, to garnish

- Pour the wine into a saucepan and add the sugar then stir over a low heat until the sugar has dissolved.
- Turn up the heat and bring to a simmer then add the cherries, put on a lid and stew gently for 10 minutes.
- Stir in the kirsch and almond essence and leave to cool. Once cooled, spoon the stewed cherries into 4 ramekins, leaving a little to garnish.
- Beat the coconut yogurt with the icing sugar until smooth then add a generous dollop on top of the cherry mixture in each ramekin.
- Garnish with a teaspoon of the cherry mixture and some crumbled biscotti for added crunch.

Stewed cherries with Greek yogurt
Replace the coconut yogurt with the same amount of Greek yogurt, for a slightly different sour taste.

Banana and almond French toast

PREPARATION TIME: **10 minutes**
COOKING TIME: **16–20 minutes**
SERVES: **4**

2 large eggs
100 ml / 3 ½ fl. oz / ½ cup milk
2 tbsp butter
8 slices white bread
2 large ripe bananas, sliced
4 tbsp maple syrup
4 tbsp flaked (slivered) almonds
icing (confectioners') sugar, to dust

- Put the oven on a low heat.
- Lightly beat the eggs with the milk in a wide, shallow dish and heat the butter in a large frying pan until sizzling.
- Dip the bread in the egg mixture on both sides until evenly coated, then fry in batches for 2 minutes on each side or until golden brown. Keep the first batches warm in the oven while you cook the rest.
- Meanwhile, put the banana slices and maple syrup in a small saucepan and warm through gently.
- When the toast is ready, spoon over the maple bananas and sprinkle with flaked almonds and a little icing sugar.

Vanilla French toast
Combine a teaspoon of vanilla powder with 1 tablespoon of icing sugar and dust over the French toast for a scrummy treat.

Strawberry roly poly

PREPARATION TIME: 15 minutes
COOKING TIME: 15–20 minutes
SERVES: 6

100 g / 3 ½ oz / ⅔ cup self-raising flour
1 tsp baking powder
100 g / 3 ½ oz / ½ cup caster (superfine) sugar
100 g / 3 ½ oz/ ½ cup butter
2 large eggs
1 tsp vanilla extract
350 g / 12 oz / 1 ½ cups strawberry jam (jelly)
350 g / 12 oz / 1 ½ cups clotted cream
icing (confectioners') sugar, to serve

- Preheat the oven to 180°C (160°C fan) / 350F / gas 4 and grease and line a Swiss roll tin.
- Put all the ingredients, except the jam and clotted cream, in a large mixing bowl and whisk together with an electric whisk for 4 minutes or until pale and well whipped.
- Spoon the mixture into the tin and spread into an even layer with a palette knife.
- Bake for 15–20 minutes or until the cake is springy to the touch.
- Turn the cake out onto a sheet of greaseproof paper.
- Spread the cake with a layer of jam and clotted cream then roll it up tightly and sieve some icing sugar to serve.

Raspberry roly poly
Replace the strawberry jam (jelly) with the same amount of raspberry jam (jelly) for an irresistible alternative.

Dried apricot rice pudding

PREPARATION TIME: **5 minutes**
COOKING TIME: **1 hour, 30 minutes**
SERVES: **4**

50 g / 1 ¾ oz / ¼ cup butter
110 g / 4 oz / ½ cup short grain rice
75 g / 2 ⅔ oz / ⅓ cup caster (superfine) sugar
1 vanilla pod, seeds only
1.2 litres / 2 pints 4 fl. oz / 4 ¾ cups whole milk
4 tbsp dried apricots, chopped

- Preheat the oven to 140°C (120°C fan) / 275F / gas 1.
- Melt the butter in a cast-iron casserole dish and add the rice, sugar and vanilla seeds.
- Stir over a low heat for 2 minutes then gradually incorporate the milk and bring to a simmer.
- Cover the casserole dish and bake in the oven for 1 hour 30 minutes.
- Spoon the rice pudding into 4 ramekins and top each one with some chopped dried apricots.

Apricot and cardamom rice pudding
Add 2 teaspoons of ground cardamom to the casserole dish with the rice, sugar and vanilla seeds.

Cherry clafoutis

PREPARATION TIME: **15 minutes**
COOKING TIME: **50 minutes**
SERVES: **8**

150 g / 5 oz / ⅔ cup butter
4 tbsp granulated sugar
600 ml / 1 pint 2 fl. oz / 2 ½ cups whole milk
4 large eggs
100 g / 3 ½ oz / ⅔ cup plain (all-purpose) flour
4 tbsp ground almonds
125 g / 4 ⅓ oz / ½ cup caster (superfine) sugar
300 g / 10 ½ oz / 2 cups cherries, stalks removed and stoned
1 tbsp caster (superfine) sugar for sprinkling

- Preheat the oven to 190°C (170°C fan) / 375F / gas 5 and line a 23 cm (9 in) spring-form cake tin with greaseproof paper.
- Melt the butter in a saucepan and cook over a low heat until it starts to smell nutty.
- Brush a little of the butter around the inside of the cake tin then add the granulated sugar and shake to coat the tin.
- Whisk together the milk and eggs with the rest of the butter.
- Sift the flour into a mixing bowl with a pinch of salt, then stir in the ground almonds and the caster sugar.
- Make a well in the middle of the dry ingredients and gradually whisk in the liquid, incorporating all the flour from round the outside until you have a lump-free batter.
- Arrange the cherries in the prepared cake tin, pour over the batter and sprinkle with the caster sugar.
- Bake the clafoutis for 50 minutes until cooked through. Leave to cool completely before unmoulding and slicing.

Rich chocolate and hazelnut torte

PREPARATION TIME: 20 minutes
COOKING TIME: 45 minutes
SERVES: 8

300 g / 10 ½ oz / 2 ½ cups hazelnuts (cob nuts)
250 g / 9 oz / 1 ¼ cups caster (superfine) sugar
1 tsp ground cinnamon
3 large eggs, separated
4 tbsp unsweetened cocoa powder
4 tbsp chopped hazelnuts (cob nuts), to serve

Rich chocolate and pecan torte
Replace the hazelnuts (cob nuts) for the same amount
of pecans. The caster sugar can also be swapped out
for 6 tablespoons of maple syrup.

- Preheat the oven to 160°C (140°C fan) / 325F / gas 3 and
  line a 23 cm (9 in) round spring-form cake tin with
  greaseproof paper.
- Put the hazelnuts in a food processor with 3 tablespoons
  of the sugar and the cinnamon and process until finely
  ground.
- Put the rest of the sugar in a bowl with the egg yolks
  and whisk with an electric whisk for 4 minutes or until
  the mixture is thick and creamy. Fold in the ground
  hazelnuts and 3 tablespoons of the cocoa powder.
- Whisk the egg whites to stiff peaks in a separate bowl,
  making sure that the bowl and whisk are clean.
- Stir a big spoonful of egg white into the torte mixture
  then fold in the rest, retaining as much air as possible.
- Scrape into the prepared tin and bake for 45 minutes.
- Transfer the tin to a wire rack and leave to cool
  completely before unmoulding.
- Sieve the remaining cocoa powder on top of the cake
  with the chopped hazelnuts before serving.

Mango tart

PREPARATION TIME: **40 minutes**
COOKING TIME: **15 minutes**
SERVES: **8**

3 tbsp butter, softened and cubed
4 tbsp soft light brown sugar
2 mangos, peeled, stoned and finely sliced
110 g / 4 oz / ½ cup butter, cubed and chilled
225 g / 8 oz / 1 ½ cups plain (all-purpose) flour

- Dot the butter over the base of a large ovenproof frying pan and sprinkle with sugar, then arrange the mango on top. Leave to infuse and cook through for 10 minutes.

- To make the pastry, rub the butter into the flour then add just enough cold water to bind the mixture together into a dough.

- Roll out the pastry on a floured surface and use it to line a 23 cm (9 in) round or ridged tart case.

- Leave the pastry to chill for 30 minutes.

- Preheat the oven to 200°C (180°C fan) / 400F / gas 6.

- Line the pastry case with oven-safe cling film and fill it with baking beans, then blind bake for 15 minutes.

- Remove the cling film and beans and return to the oven until golden brown and crisp. Leave to cool.

- Spoon the mango slices into the tart case, layering the pieces carefully to ensure the flesh is evenly spread. Leave to cool at room temperature and then serve.

Orange crème caramel

PREPARATION TIME: 15 minutes
COOKING TIME: 25 minutes
CHILLING TIME: overnight
SERVES: 6

175 g / 6 oz / ¾ cup caster (superfine) sugar
1 tbsp butter, softened
500 ml / 17 ½ fl. oz / 2 cups whole milk
100 ml / 3 ½ fl. oz / ½ cup orange juice, sieved
4 large eggs
1 tsp orange zest, finely grated
1 tbsp triple sec
6 fresh raspberries, to garnish
6 fresh mint leaves, to garnish

Coffee crème caramel
A great dessert for coffee lovers. Add 2 shots of
espresso to the caramel mixture before pouring
the contents into individual ramekins. Garnish the
caramels with some shaved dark chocolate.

- Preheat the oven to 150°C (130°C fan) / 300F / gas 2.
- Put 150 g / 5 oz / ⅔ cup of the caster sugar in a heavy-based saucepan and heat gently until it starts to turn liquid at the edges. Continue to heat and swirl the pan until the sugar has melted and turned golden brown.
- Divide the caramel between 6 ramekin dishes and leave to set, then butter the sides of the ramekins.
- Whisk the rest of the ingredients with the remaining caster sugar and divide between the ramekins.
- Sit the ramekins in a roasting tin and pour boiling water around them to come halfway up their sides.
- Transfer the tin to the oven and bake for 25 minutes or until they are just set in the middle. Remove the ramekins from the tray and chill overnight.
- Give the ramekins a shake to loosen the crème caramels, then turn each one out onto a plate.
- Garnish each crème caramel with a raspberry and mint leaf. Serve immediately.

Nutty chocolate fudge

PREPARATION TIME: 10 minutes
COOKING TIME: 45 minutes
MAKES: 36

300 ml / 10 ½ fl. oz / 1 ¼ cups whole milk
100 g / 3 ½ oz / ½ cup butter
350 g / 12 oz / 1 ½ cups caster (superfine) sugar
3 tbsp unsweetened cocoa powder
100 g / 3 ½ oz / ¾ cup walnuts, roughly chopped
1 jar smooth peanut butter

Hazelnut and raisin fudge
Replace the walnuts with the same amount of
hazelnuts (cob nuts) and add 100 g / 3 ½ oz / ½ cup
raisins to the mixture before leaving it to set.

- Oil an 18 cm (7 in) square cake tin.
- Put the milk, butter, caster sugar and cocoa in a large, heavy-based saucepan and stir over a low heat to dissolve the sugar.
- Increase the temperature a little and bring to the boil.
- Boil the mixture for 35 minutes or until it reaches 115°C / 240F on a sugar thermometer, stirring constantly.
- Take the pan off the heat and stir in the walnut pieces and the peanut butter, then continue to stir for a further 10 minutes while it cools.
- Scrape the mixture into the prepared tin and level the surface with a palate knife.
- Leave the fudge to cool completely, then turn it out of the tin and cut it into 36 squares with a sharp knife.

Blueberry and banana meringue pies

PREPARATION TIME: 40 minutes
COOKING TIME: 30 minutes
MAKES: 4

100 g / 3 ½ oz / ½ cup butter, cubed
200 g / 7 oz / 1 ⅓ cups plain (all-purpose) flour
4 large ripe bananas
1 lime, juiced
75 g / 2 ⅔ oz / ½ cup fresh blueberries
fresh mint, to garnish (optional)

FOR THE MERINGUE
4 large eggs, separated, whites
110 g / 4 oz / ½ cup caster (superfine) sugar

- Preheat the oven to 200°C (180°C fan) / 400F / gas 6.
- Rub butter into the flour and add cold water to bind into a dough.
- Chill for 30 minutes then roll out on a floured surface. Line 4 tart cases with pastry and prick the bases.
- Line the pastry cases with oven-safe cling film and fill with baking beans then blind bake for 10 minutes.
- Remove the cling film and beans and cook for a further 8 minutes.
- Mash the bananas with the lime juice until smooth then stir in half of the blueberries.
- Divide the mixture between the pastry cases.
- Whisk the egg whites until stiff then add the sugar. Whisk until the mixture is thick and shiny.
- Spoon into a piping bag and pipe the meringue onto the tarts.
- Return the tarts to the oven and bake for 10 minutes.
- Sprinkle over the remaining blueberries and serve with some fresh mint.

Chocolate and banana meringue pies
Replace the blueberries with the same amount of dark chocolate chips for a more decadent variation.

Chocolate brownies

PREPARATION TIME: **15 minutes**
COOKING TIME: **35–40 minutes**
SERVES: **8**

110 g / 4 oz milk chocolate, chopped
85 g / 3 oz / ½ cup unsweetened cocoa powder, sifted
225 g / 8 oz / 1 cup butter
450 g / 1 lb / 2 ½ cups light brown sugar
4 large eggs
110 g / 4 oz / ⅔ cup self-raising flour
75 g / 2 ⅔ oz / ⅔ cup pistachio nuts, chopped
75 g / 2 ⅔ oz / ⅔ cup walnuts, chopped
icing (confectioners') sugar, for dusting
mint ice cream, to serve (optional)

- Preheat the oven to 160°C (140°C fan) / 325F / gas 3 and oil and line a 20 cm x 20 cm (8 in x 8 in) square cake tin.
- Melt the chocolate, cocoa and butter together in a saucepan, then leave to cool a little.
- Whisk the sugar and eggs together with an electric whisk for 3 minutes or until very light and creamy.
- Pour in the chocolate mixture and sieve over the flour, then fold everything together with the nuts until evenly mixed.
- Scrape into the tin and bake for 35–40 minutes or until the outside is set, but the middle is still quite soft.
- Leave the brownie to cool completely before cutting into 8 rectangles and dusting with icing sugar.
- Serve with mint ice cream.

Chocolate and vanilla tiramisu

PREPARATION TIME: **30 minutes**
CHILLING TIME: **4 hours**
SERVES: **6**

600 ml / 1 pint 2 fl. oz / 2 ½ cups double (heavy) cream
300 g / 10 ½ oz / 1 ¼ cups mascarpone
4 tbsp icing (confectioners') sugar
1 vanilla pod, seeds extracted and finely chopped
100 ml / 3 ½ fl. oz / ½ cup Marsala
300 g / 10 ½ oz sponge fingers
unsweetened cocoa powder, for dusting

- Put the cream, mascarpone, sugar and vanilla seeds in a bowl with half of the Marsala and whip with an electric whisk until it holds its shape.
- Divide a quarter of the mixture between 6 individual ramekins and top with half of the sponge fingers.
- Sprinkle the tiramisus with half of the remaining Marsala, then spread with another quarter of the mascarpone mixture on top.
- Lay the rest of the sponge fingers on top and press down lightly.
- Drizzle over the rest of the Marsala and spread with another quarter of the mascarpone.
- Spoon the rest of the mascarpone on top of each individual pudding.
- Dust the tiramisu with cocoa and chill in the fridge for 4 hours. Serve chilled.

Chocolate and cardamom tiramisu
Replace the vanilla seeds with half a teaspoon of ground cardamom and whip with an electric whisk. Dust the tiramisus with a combination of cocoa and ground cardamom, then serve.

Plum clafoutis

PREPARATION TIME: 20 minutes
COOKING TIME: 25 minutes
SERVES: 4

75 g / 2 ⅔ oz / ⅓ cup butter
75 g / 2 ⅔ oz / ⅓ cup caster (superfine) sugar
300 ml / 10 fl. oz / 1 ¼ cups whole milk
2 large eggs
50 g / 1 ¾ oz / ⅓ cup plain (all-purpose) flour
2 tbsp ground almonds
4 plums, stones removed and sliced
icing (confectioners') sugar, to serve

- Preheat the oven to 190°C (170°C fan) / 375F / gas 5.
- Melt the butter in a saucepan and cook over a low heat until it starts to smell nutty.

- Brush a little of the butter around the inside of 4 gratin dishes then sprinkle with a little caster sugar and shake to coat.
- Whisk together the milk and eggs with the rest of the butter. Sift the flour into a mixing bowl with a pinch of salt, then stir in the ground almonds and the rest of the sugar.
- Make a well in the middle of the dry ingredients and gradually whisk in the liquid, incorporating all the flour from round the outside until you have a lump-free batter.
- Arrange half of the plum slices in the prepared dishes, then pour in the batter. Add the remaining plum slices on top.
- Bake the clafoutis for 25 minutes or until cooked through.
- Dust each one with icing sugar, then serve immediately.

Cherry tart

PREPARATION TIME: **10 minutes**
COOKING TIME: **25 minutes**
SERVES: **4**

250 g / 9 oz all-butter puff pastry
1 egg, beaten
300 g / 10 ½ oz / 2 cups cherries, stalks removed,
stoned and halved
2 tbsp caster (superfine) sugar
icing (confectioners') sugar, to dust

- Preheat the oven to 220°C (200°C fan) / 425F / gas 7.
- Roll out the pastry on a floured surface into a circle.
- Transfer the pastry to a baking sheet and brush with
  beaten egg then arrange the cherry halves on top, flat
  side down.
- Sprinkle with sugar, then transfer the tray to the oven
  and bake for 25 minutes or until the pastry is golden
  brown and cooked through.
- Once cooked, remove from the oven and sprinkle with
  a little icing sugar. Serve warm.

Melon granita

PREPARATION TIME: **30 minutes**
FREEZING TIME: **5 hours**
SERVES: **18**

2 very ripe Charentais melons, halved
1 tbsp melon liqueur
a handful of fresh blueberries, to garnish
fresh mint leaves, to garnish

- Scoop out and discard the seeds of the melons,
  then use a spoon to scrape out the flesh,
  discarding the empty shells.
- Roughly chop the flesh and put it in a freezer
  bag, then freeze for 4 hours or until solid.
- Transfer the frozen melon to a food processor
  and process for 2 minutes.
- Add the melon liqueur and process to the
  consistency of granita.
- Spoon the granita into a plastic tub with a lid
  and freeze for 1 hour.
- Serve with some fresh blueberries and mint
  leaves on the side.

Melon sorbet
Blend 1 lightly beaten egg white with the melon
and liqueur until smooth then follow the method
above for a delicious creamy sorbet.

Blackberry and apple crumble

PREPARATION TIME: 20 minutes
COOKING TIME: 40 minutes
SERVES: 6

450 g / 1 lb / 3 cups blackberries, defrosted if frozen
2 large cooking apples, peeled, cored and sliced
4 tbsp caster (superfine) sugar
75 g / 2 ⅔ oz / ⅓ cup butter
50 g / 1 ¾ oz / ⅓ cup plain (all-purpose) flour
1 ½ tbsp ground almonds
3 tbsp light brown sugar

- Preheat the oven to 180°C (160°C fan) / 350F / gas 4.
- Mix the blackberries and apple with the caster sugar and arrange in an even layer in the bottom of a baking dish.
- Rub the butter into the flour and stir in the ground almonds and brown sugar.
- Squeeze a handful of the mixture into a clump and then crumble it over the fruit. Use up the rest of the topping in the same way, then shake the dish to level the top.
- Bake the crumble for 40 minutes or until the topping is golden brown and the fruit is bubbling.

Blackberry and pear crumbles
Replace the apple with the same amount of pear. Simply peel and chop 2 large conference pears and follow the method as above.

Chocolate and banana parfait

PREPARATION TIME: 35–40 minutes
SERVES: 4

4 tbsp chia seeds
4 tbsp maple syrup
1 tsp vanilla powder
1.2 litres / 2 pints 4 fl. oz / 4 ¾ cups almond milk
4 dates, stoned
2 tbsp cacao powder
2 bananas, mashed
a handful of granola, to garnish
2 bananas, sliced, to garnish

- Combine the chia seeds, 2 tablespoons of maple syrup, vanilla powder and half the milk in a large bowl. Mix thoroughly and leave in the fridge for 30 minutes to set.
- Blend the dates with the remaining maple syrup, cacao powder and the rest of the milk. Divide the chocolate mixture between 4 serving glasses.
- Mash 2 bananas with the back of a fork and spoon a little on top of the chocolate layer.
- Once the chia seeds have expanded and the chilled mixture has doubled in size, divide between the 4 serving glasses to make the third layer.
- Sprinkle some granola and sliced banana on top.

Very berry chocolate parfait
Replace the mashed banana layer with frozen berries and the chopped banana with a handful of fresh mixed berries.

Coffee and chocolate muffins

PREPARATION TIME: **10 minutes**
COOKING TIME: **20–25 minutes**
MAKES: **12**

1 large egg
120 ml / 4 ¼ fl. oz / ½ cup coconut oil, melted
120 ml / 4 ¼ fl. oz / ½ cup milk
375 g / 13 oz / 2 ½ cups self-raising flour, sifted
1 tsp baking powder
200 g / 7 oz / ¾ cup caster (superfine) sugar
1 tbsp instant espresso powder
75 g / 2 ⅔ oz / ½ cup chocolate chips

- Preheat the oven to 180°C (160°C fan) / 350F / gas 4 and line a 12-hole muffin tin with paper cases.
- Beat the egg in a jug with the oil and milk until well mixed.
- Mix the flour, baking powder, sugar, espresso powder and chocolate chips in a bowl, then pour in the egg mixture and stir just enough to combine.
- Spoon the mixture into the cases, then bake in the oven for 20–25 minutes.
- Test with a wooden toothpick, if it comes out clean, the muffins are done.
- Transfer the muffins to a wire rack and leave to cool completely.

Vanilla and chocolate muffins
Replace the instant espresso powder with 1 tablespoon of vanilla powder for a classic alternative.

Classic treacle tart

PREPARATION TIME: **40 minutes**
COOKING TIME: **25–30 minutes**
SERVES: **8**

350 g / 12 oz / 1 cup golden syrup
2 lemons, zest and juice
100 g / 3 ½ oz / 1 ⅓ cups wholemeal breadcrumbs
clotted cream, to serve

FOR THE PASTRY
100 g / 3 ½ oz / ½ cup butter, cubed and chilled
200 g / 7 oz / 1 ⅓ cups wholemeal flour

- Preheat the oven to 200°C (180°C fan) / 400F
  / gas 6.
- First make the pastry. Rub the butter into
  the flour until the mixture resembles fine
  breadcrumbs.
- Stir in just enough cold water to bring the
  pastry together into a dough then chill for
  30 minutes.
- Heat the golden syrup with the lemon
  zest and juice until runny then stir in the
  breadcrumbs.
- Roll out the pastry on a floured surface and
  use it to line a 23 cm (9 in) round tart case.
- Spoon the filling into the pastry case and
  level the top.
- Bake for 25–30 minutes or until the pastry is
  cooked through underneath.
- Serve warm with clotted cream.

Lemon and lime treacle tart
Add the zest and juice of a lime to the syrup
mixture and sprinkle some lemon and lime zest
over the finish tart.

Waffles with blueberry compote

PREPARATION TIME: 10 minutes
COOKING TIME: 20–25 minutes
SERVES: 4

250 g / 9 oz / 1 ⅔ cups plain (all-purpose) flour
2 tsp baking powder
2 large eggs
300 ml / 10 fl. oz / 1 ¼ cups milk
2 tbsp butter, melted
sunflower oil, for oiling the waffle maker
blueberry compote, to serve
a handful of fresh blueberries, to serve
icing (confectioners') sugar, to serve

- Put the oven on a low setting and put an electric waffle maker on to heat up.
- Mix the flour and baking powder in a bowl and make a well in the middle.
- Break in the eggs and pour in the milk then use a whisk to gradually incorporate all the flour from round the outside, followed by the melted butter.
- Spoon some of the batter into the waffle maker and close the lid. Cook for 4 minutes, or according to the manufacturer's instructions, until golden brown.
- Repeat until all the batter has been used, keeping the finished batches warm in the oven.
- Put a generous dollop of blueberry compote on each stack of waffles and sprinkle over some fresh blueberries. Dust the waffles liberally with icing sugar, then serve.

Chocolate fondants with strawberries

PREPARATION TIME: **50 minutes**
COOKING TIME: **8 minutes**
SERVES: **6**

2 tbsp unsweetened cocoa powder
150 g / 5 oz milk chocolate, chopped
150 g / 5 oz / ⅔ cup butter, chopped
85 g / 3 oz / ⅓ cup caster (superfine) sugar
3 large eggs, plus 3 egg yolks
1 tbsp plain (all-purpose) flour
12 strawberries, halved
fresh mint leaves, to garnish
icing (confectioners') sugar, for dusting

- Oil 6 mini pudding basins and dust the insides with cocoa.
- Melt the chocolate, butter and sugar together in a saucepan, stirring to dissolve the sugar.
- Leave to cool a little then beat in the eggs and egg yolks and fold in the flour.
- Divide the mixture between the pudding basins then chill them for 30 minutes.
- Preheat the oven to 180°C (160°C fan) / 350F / gas 4 and put a baking tray in to heat.
- Transfer the fondants to the heated baking tray and bake in the oven for 8 minutes.
- Leave the fondants to cool for 2 minutes. Add the strawberries and mint leaves on top of each fondant and sprinkle with icing sugar. Serve immediately.

Dark chocolate fondants
For a rich and decadent dessert, swap the milk chocolate for the same amount of dark chocolate with a minimum of 70% cocoa solids.

Blueberry lollies

PREPARATION TIME: **5 minutes**
FREEZING TIME: **Overnight**
MAKES: **10 lollies**

1 punnet fresh blueberries, washed
400 ml / 14 fl. oz can coconut milk
4 tbsp agave nectar
1 tbsp acai powder

- Blend or mash the blueberries using the back of a fork or potato masher.
- Combine all the ingredients in a large mixing bowl. Mix together until well incorporated.
- Divide the mixture between the ice-lolly moulds and insert a stick into the middle of each.
- Leave overnight to freeze.

Summer trifle pots

PREPARATION TIME: **25 minutes**
SERVES: **8**

450 ml / 16 fl. oz / 1 ¾ cups double (heavy) cream
4 tbsp icing (confectioners') sugar
1 tsp vanilla extract
8 tbsp strawberry jam (jelly)
150 g / 5 oz / 1 cup strawberries, chopped
basil leaves, to garnish

- Whip the cream with the icing sugar and vanilla extract until it forms soft peaks.
- Divide half of the strawberry jam between the 8 glasses. Add half of the cream, then scatter over half of the chopped strawberries.
- Repeat with the rest of the jam, cream and fruit, then top with the basil leaves and refrigerate until ready to serve.

Gooseberry pots
Replace the strawberry jam (jelly) and fresh strawberries with the same amount of gooseberry jam (jelly) and very ripe fresh gooseberries for a sharper taste.

Blueberry and coconut pancakes

PREPARATION TIME: 10 Minutes
COOKING TIME: 30 Minutes
SERVES: 4

250 g / 9 oz / 1 ⅔ cups plain (all-purpose) flour
2 tsp baking powder
2 large eggs
300 ml / 10 ½ fl. oz / 1 ½ cups coconut milk
2 tbsp coconut oil
2 tbsp shredded coconut, plus extra to serve
a handful of fresh blueberries, to garnish
icing (confectioners') sugar, to dust (optional)

- Mix the flour and baking powder in a bowl and make a well in the centre.
- Break in the eggs and pour in the coconut milk then use a whisk to gradually incorporate all of the flour from around the outside.
- Melt the oil in a small frying pan then whisk it into the batter with the shredded coconut.
- Put the buttered frying pan back over a low heat. You will need a tablespoon of batter for each pancake and you should be able to cook 4 pancakes at a time in the frying pan.
- Spoon the batter into the pan and cook for 2 minutes or until small bubbles start to appear on the surface.
- Turn the pancakes over with a spatula and cook the other side until golden brown.
- Repeat until all the batter has been used, keeping the finished batches warm in a low oven.
- Pile the pancakes onto warm plates and sprinkle with some more shredded coconut and blueberries. Sift some icing sugar on top for extra sweetness.

Almond and coconut pancakes
Replace the coconut milk with the same amount of almond milk. To garnish, sprinkle some toasted flaked almonds on top and drizzle over some maple syrup.

Peach, vanilla and almond crumble

PREPARATION TIME: **15 minutes**
COOKING TIME: **40 minutes**
SERVES: **4**

4 peaches, peeled, stoned and cubed
75 g / 2 ⅔ oz / ⅓ cup butter
50 g / 1 ¾ oz / ⅓ cup plain (all-purpose) flour
1 tbsp ground almonds
1 ½ tbsp light brown sugar
½ tsp vanilla powder
4 tbsp flaked (slivered) almonds
vanilla ice cream (optional)

- Preheat the oven to 180°C (160°C fan) / 350F / gas 4.
- Arrange the cubed peaches in a baking dish.
- Rub the butter into the flour and stir in the ground almonds, sugar and vanilla powder.
- Take a handful of the topping and squeeze it into a clump, then crumble it over the fruit.
- Repeat with the rest of the crumble mixture then sprinkle the flaked almonds on top.
- Bake for 40 minutes or until the topping is golden brown.
- Serve with some vanilla ice cream on the side (optional).

Creamy avocado mousse

PREPARATION TIME: **15 minutes**
SERVES: **4**

2 Hass avocados, stones removed and halved
2 tbsp maple syrup
1 tsp vanilla powder
1 tsp ground cinnamon
4 dates, stones removed
½ tsp salt
4 tbsp water
1 banana, sliced
a handful of cashew nuts, chopped

- Add the avocado, maple syrup, vanilla powder, cinnamon, dates, salt and water to a blender. Blend until creamy and add a little more water if necessary.
- Divide the mousse between 4 glasses.
- Garnish with the banana slices and cashews. Serve cold.

Double-choc avocado mousse
Grate some dark chocolate on top and sprinkle over some cacao nibs for a scrummy chocolate hit!

Chocolate and vanilla custard pots

PREPARATION TIME: 10 minutes
COOKING TIME: 15 minutes
CHILLING TIME: 1 hour, 30 minutes
SERVES: 6

450 ml / 16 fl. oz / 1 ¾ cups whole milk
4 large egg yolks
75 g / 2 ⅔ oz / ⅓ cup caster (superfine) sugar
1 tsp cornflour (cornstarch)
1 tsp vanilla extract
1 vanilla pod, seeds extracted and finely chopped
2 tbsp unsweetened cocoa powder

- Put the milk in a saucepan and bring to simmering point.
- Whisk the egg yolks with the caster sugar, cornflour, vanilla extract, vanilla seeds until thick.
- Gradually incorporate the hot milk, whisking all the time, then scrape the mixture back into the saucepan.
- Stir the custard over a low heat until it thickens, then reserve a third of the mixture in a separate pan.
- Add the cocoa powder to the larger quantity of custard and stir until thick. Divide the chocolate custard between 6 small glass ramekins.
- Chill in the fridge for 30 minutes, then divide the remaining vanilla custard between the 6 ramekins and chill for 1 hour or until firm, then serve.

Hot chocolate and vanilla pots
This recipe can also be served hot. Incorporate the same amount of cocoa powder at an earlier stage and spoon the mixture into the ramekins. Grate some white or dark chocolate on top and serve.

Strawberry vanilla panna cotta

PREPARATION TIME: **10 minutes**
COOKING TIME: **10 minutes**
SERVES: **6**

150 g / 5 oz strawberries, halved
1 tbsp vanilla sugar
450 ml / 16 fl. oz / 1 ¾ cups whole milk
4 large egg yolks
75 g / 2 ⅔ oz / ⅓ cup caster (superfine) sugar
1 tsp cornflour (cornstarch)
1 tsp vanilla extract

- Reserve 6 strawberry halves for decoration then toss the rest with the vanilla sugar and divide between 6 shallow dishes.
- Put the milk in a saucepan and bring to simmering point.
- Whisk the egg yolks with the caster sugar, cornflour and vanilla extract until thick.
- Gradually incorporate the hot milk, whisking all the time, then scrape the mixture back into the saucepan.
- Stir the panna cotta mixture over a low heat until it thickens, then spoon it on top of the strawberries.
- If desired, use a blowtorch to lightly brown the top of the panna cotta, then lay a strawberry slice on top and serve warm, or chilled.

Dried fig panna cotta
Replace the strawberries with chopped dried figs for a delicious variation of the classic Italian dessert.

Raspberry pudding pots

PREPARATION TIME: **10 minutes**
COOKING TIME: **25 minutes**
SERVES: **6**

4 large eggs
75 g / 2 ⅔ oz / ⅓ cup caster (superfine) sugar
1 tsp cornflour (cornstarch)
1 tsp vanilla extract
450 ml / 16 fl. oz / 1 ¾ cups whole milk
150 g / 5 oz / 1 cup fresh raspberries
6 tbsp raspberry jam (jelly)
fresh lemon verbena leaves, to garnish

- Whisk the eggs with the caster sugar, cornflour and vanilla extract until thick.
- Gradually incorporate the milk, whisking all the time, then stir in half the raspberries and divide between 6 small jars.
- Bake in the oven at 180°C (160°C fan) / 350F / gas 4 for 25 minutes, or until a skewer inserted into the middle comes out clean.
- Top each one with a dollop of raspberry jam, the remaining fresh raspberries and some lemon verbena.
- Serve warm, or chill in the fridge for 2 hours and serve cold.

Summer berry pudding pots
Replace the raspberries for the same amount of summer berries (blackcurrants, strawberries, blackberries) and garnish with a mixed berry jam (jelly).

No-cook cacao cookies

PREPARATION TIME: **20 minutes**
CHILLING TIME: **30 minutes**
MAKES: **8**

50 g / 1 ¾ oz / ½ cup almonds
50 g / 1 ¾ oz / ½ cup walnuts
8 dates, stones removed
1 tbsp coconut oil, melted
1 pinch salt
2 tbsp water

FOR THE TOPPING
1 tbsp coconut oil, melted
1 tbsp maple syrup
1 tbsp cacao powder
1 pinch sea salt
8 walnut halves

- Add all the cookie ingredients to a food processor and blend until a sticky dough is formed. Add a little more water if necessary.
- Use an ice-cream scoop or tablespoon to spoon out the mixture and roll into a cookie shape.
- To make the topping, add 2.5 cm (1 in) of water to a saucepan and bring to the boil. Sit a heatproof glass bowl on top, ensuring the bowl doesn't touch the water.
- Add the coconut oil, followed by the maple syrup and then slowly stir in the cacao powder and salt. Once the mixture is a velvety smooth consistency, remove from the heat and set to one side.
- Spoon a little chocolate sauce to the top of each cookie and then place a walnut firmly on top.
- Put the cookies in the fridge for 30 minutes or until the chocolate sauce has solidified.

No-cook goji cookies
Replace the walnut halves with a few goji berries. Simply sprinkle on top of the chocolate sauce and leave in the fridge to set as normal.

Melt-in-the-middle puddings

PREPARATION TIME: **10 Minutes**
COOKING TIME: **35-40 Minutes**
SERVES: **8**

200 g / 7 oz / 1 ⅓ cups self-raising flour
200 g / 7 oz / ½ cup dark brown sugar
200 g / 7 oz / ½ cup butter
4 large eggs
1 tsp baking powder
3 tbsp unsweetened cocoa powder
fresh mint leaves, to garnish

FOR THE SAUCE
200 ml / 7 fl. oz / ½ cup double (heavy) cream
200 g / 7 oz dark chocolate, min. 60% cocoa solids, chopped

- Butter 8 individual pudding basins and put a steamer on to heat.
- Put all of the cake ingredients in a large mixing bowl and whisk with an electric whisk for 4 minutes.
- Divide the mixture between the pudding basins then transfer them to the steamer and steam for 1 hour.
- Heat the cream until it starts to simmer but not boiling, then pour it over the chopped chocolate and stir continuously until smooth.
- Carefully unmould the puddings onto warm plates and make a shallow hole in the top of each pudding. Carefully pour the sauce into the hole and allow it to spill out onto the plate.
- Garnish with some fresh mint leaves.

Mint chocolate puddings
Add a few drops of natural peppermint essence to the chocolate sauce ingredients for a subtle minty flavour.

Peanut butter cheesecake

PREPARATION TIME: 20 minutes
COOKING TIME: 40–50 minutes
CHILLING TIME: 3 hours
SERVES: 12

600 g / 1 lb 5 oz / 2 ½ cups cream cheese
150 ml / 5 ⅓ fl. oz / ⅔ cup double cream
175 g / 6 oz / ¾ cup caster (superfine) sugar
2 large eggs, plus 1 egg yolk
2 tbsp plain (all-purpose) flour

FOR THE BASE
200 g / 7 oz digestive biscuits, crushed
50 g / 1 ¾ oz / ¼ cup smooth peanut butter

FOR THE TOPPING
100 g / 3 ½ oz plain chocolate, melted
150 g / 5 oz / 1 ¼ cups salted peanuts, roughly chopped

- Preheat the oven to 180°C (160°C fan) / 350F / gas 4 and grease a 20 cm (8 in) round spring-form cake tin.
- To make the base, mix the biscuit crumbs with the peanut butter and press into an even layer in the bottom of the tin.
- Bake the biscuit layer for 5 minutes or until firm.
- Whisk together the filling ingredients until smooth.
- Spoon the cheesecake mixture on top of the biscuit base, levelling the top with a palette knife.
- Bake the cheesecake for 40–50 minutes or until the middle is only just set.
- Leave to cool completely in the tin, then drizzle the melted chocolate on top and sprinkle on some peanuts.
- Chill for at least 3 hours before serving.

Coffee and peanut butter cheesecake
Add 2 teaspoons of coffee liqueur to the filling ingredients and whisk thoroughly for a rich coffee taste.

Coffee banoffee pie

PREPARATION TIME: 3 hours, 50 minutes
COOKING TIME: 20 minutes
SERVES: 12

400 g / 14 oz can condensed milk
110 g / 4 oz / ½ cup butter, cubed and chilled
225 g / 8 oz / 1 ½ cups plain (all-purpose) flour
3 bananas, chopped
300 ml / 10 fl. oz / 1 ¼ cups double (heavy) cream
2 tbsp ground coffee, to garnish

- Put the unopened can of condensed milk in a saucepan of water and simmer for 3 hours, adding more water as necessary to ensure it doesn't boil dry. Leave to cool completely.

- Rub the butter into the flour then add just enough cold water to bind the mixture together into a dough.
- Roll out the pastry on a floured surface and use it to line a 23 cm (9 in) round tart case.
- Leave the pastry to chill for 30 minutes.
- Preheat the oven to 200°C (180°C fan) / 400F / gas 6.
- Line the pastry case with oven-safe cling film and fill it with baking beans, then blind bake for 15 minutes.
- Remove the cling film and beans and return to the oven until golden brown and crisp. Leave to cool.
- Open the can of condensed milk and beat the caramel until smooth then stir in the banana.
- Spoon the mixture into the pastry case and level the top.
- Whip the cream until it holds its shape, then spoon on top of the caramel layer. Sprinkle over a little ground coffee, to garnish.

Strawberry granita

PREPARATION TIME: **10 minutes**
FREEZING TIME: **5 hours**
SERVES: **10**

450 g / 1 lb strawberries, washed
175 g / 6 oz / ¾ cup caster (superfine) sugar
3 tbsp fresh lemon juice
fresh mint leaves, to garnish

- Place the strawberries in a freezer bag, then freeze for 4 hours or until solid.
- Transfer the frozen strawberries to a food processor and process for 2 minutes.
- Add the sugar and lemon juice and process to the consistency of granita.
- Spoon the granita into a plastic tub with a lid and freeze for 1 hour.
- Serve with some fresh mint leaves on the side.

Cacao chia pudding

PREPARATION TIME: **Overnight**
SERVES: **2**

4 tbsp chia seeds
240 ml / 8 ½ fl. oz / 1 cup almond milk
240 g / 8 ½ oz / 2 ½ cups rolled oats
2 tbsp cacao powder
2 tbsp maple syrup
a handful of black seedless grapes, sliced
1 banana, sliced
2 tbsp desiccated coconut, to garnish

- Mix the chia seeds with the almond milk and leave in the fridge overnight to set.
- Once set, mix in the oats, cacao powder and maple syrup.
- Divide the chia pudding between 2 small bowls and top with the grapes, banana and coconut.
- Serve cold.

Cacao nib cinnamon pudding
Add half a teaspoon of ground cinnamon to the mixture before serving. Sprinkle with some cacao nibs for added crunch.

Berry chia pudding

PREPARATION TIME: 40 minutes
SERVES: 2

400 g / 14 oz / 1 ⅔ cups Greek yogurt
2 tbsp chia seeds
4 tbsp desiccated coconut
2 tbsp maple syrup
pinch of salt
a handful of fresh mixed berries, to serve
sprig of mint, to serve

- Mix the yogurt with the chia seeds, coconut, maple syrup and a pinch of salt.
- Leave for at least 30 minutes to allow the chia seeds to expand.
- Once ready, top with the mixed berries and garnish with a sprig of mint.

Cacao berry chia pudding
Add 1 tablespoon of cacao powder to the yogurt ingredients and mix thoroughly. Sprinkle some cacao nibs on top to garnish.

Lemon rice pudding

PREPARATION TIME: 5 minutes
COOKING TIME: 1 hour, 35 minutes
SERVES: 2

50 g / 1 ⅔ oz / ¼ cup butter
110 g / 4 oz / ½ cup short grain rice
75 g / 2 ⅔ oz / ⅓ cup caster (superfine) sugar
2 lemons, zested
1.2 litres / 2 pints 4 fl. oz / 4 ¾ cups milk

- Preheat the oven to 140°C (120°C fan) / 275F / gas 1.
- Melt the butter in a cast-iron casserole dish and add the rice, sugar and lemon zest.
- Stir over a low heat for 2 minutes then incorporate the milk and bring to a simmer.
- Add the mixture to individual ramekins and bake in the oven for 1 hour 30 minutes.
- Spoon the rice pudding into mugs and garnish with some lemon zest.

Chocolate rice pudding
Add 1 tablespoon of unsweetened cocoa powder to the mixture before incorporating the milk and bringing to a simmer. Replace the lemon zest with grated dark chocolate to garnish.

Blackcurrant muffins

PREPARATION TIME: 15 minutes
COOKING TIME: 20–25 minutes
MAKES: 12

1 large egg
120 ml / 4 ¼ fl. oz / ½ cup sunflower oil
120 ml / 4 ¼ fl. oz / ½ cup milk
375 g / 13 oz / 2 ½ cups self-raising flour, sifted
1 tsp baking powder
200 g / 7 oz / ¾ cup caster (superfine) sugar
100 g / 3 ½ oz / ⅔ cup blackcurrants

- Preheat the oven to 180°C (160°C fan) / 350F / gas 4 and line a 12-hole muffin tin with paper cases.
- Beat the egg in a jug with the oil and milk until well mixed.
- Mix the flour, baking powder and sugar in a bowl.
- Pour in the egg mixture and stir just enough to combine, then fold through the blackcurrants.
- Divide the mixture between the paper cases and bake for 20–25 minutes.
- Test with a wooden toothpick. If it comes out clean, the muffins are done.
- Transfer the muffins to a wire rack and leave to cool completely.
- Serve with a few fresh blackcurrants on the side.

Blackcurrant spelt muffins
Swap the self-raising flour with equal parts of spelt flour, for a wholesome and healthy alternative.

Baked spiced apples

PREPARATION TIME: 10 minutes
COOKING TIME: 15–20 minutes
SERVES: 4

4 eating apples, peeled, halved and cored
600 ml / 1 pint 2 fl. oz / 2 ½ cups white grape juice
1 lemon, zest finely pared

FOR THE COMPOTE
100 g / 3 ½ oz / ⅔ cup cranberries
75 g / 2 ⅔ oz / ½ cup brown sugar
½ tsp ground cinnamon
1 orange, zest finely grated
100 g / 3 ½ oz / ⅔ cup chopped walnuts

- Put the apples, cut side down in a single layer in a wide sauté pan. Pour over the grape juice and sprinkle with lemon zest.
- Bring the pan to a gently simmer, then put on a lid and poach for 15 minutes.
- Meanwhile, put the cranberries in a small saucepan with the sugar, cinnamon and orange zest. Cover and cook gently for 5 minutes then remove the lid, give it a stir and cook for a further 10 minutes or until the cranberries start to burst and the juices thicken.
- Leave the cranberry compote to cool completely, then stir in the chopped walnuts.
- Turn the apples cut side up in a serving dish and spoon the compote inside.

Baked apples with maple
Replace the brown sugar with 4 tablespoons of maple syrup for a healthy version. The maple syrup and cranberries make a delicious combination.

Classic pecan pie

PREPARATION TIME: 50 minutes
COOKING TIME: 40 minutes
SERVES: 8

200 g / 7 oz / 1 ¼ cups dark brown sugar
100 g / 3 ½ oz / ⅓ cup maple syrup
100 g / 3 ½ oz / ½ cup butter
1 tsp vanilla extract
3 large eggs, beaten
3 tbsp plain (all-purpose) flour
300 g / 10 ½ oz pecan halves

FOR THE PASTRY
150 g / 5 oz / ⅔ cup butter, cubed and chilled
300 g / 10 ½ oz / 2 cups plain (all-purpose) flour

FOR THE TOFFEE SAUCE
100 g / 3 ½ oz / ½ cup butter
100 g / 3 ½ oz / ½ cup muscovado sugar
100 g / 3 ½ oz / ⅓ cup golden syrup
100 ml / 3 ½ fl. oz / ½ cup double (heavy) cream

- First make the pastry. Rub the butter into the flour then add just enough cold water to bind the mixture together into a dough.
- Roll out the pastry on a floured surface and use it to line a 23 cm (9 in) round or ridged tart case then chill for 30 minutes.
- Put all the toffee sauce ingredients in a small saucepan and stir over a low heat until the sugar dissolves. Bring to the boil then take off the heat.
- Preheat the oven to 180°C (160°C fan) / 350F / gas 4.
- Put the sugar, maple syrup, butter and vanilla extract in a saucepan and stir it over a low heat to dissolve the sugar.
- Leave the mixture to cool for 10 minutes then beat in the eggs and flour.
- Spoon the toffee sauce into the chilled pastry case then pour in the cake mixture.
- Arrange the pecans on top, then bake the tart for 40 minutes.
- Leave the tart to cool, then transfer to a serving plate.

Toffee walnut pie
Replace the pecan halves with the same quantity of walnut halves for an unusual take on the American classic.

Hot chocolate profiteroles

PREPARATION TIME: 20 minutes
COOKING TIME: 20 minutes
MAKES: 24

55 g / 2 oz / ¼ cup butter, cubed
75 g / 2 ⅔ oz / ½ cup strong white bread flour, sifted
2 large eggs, beaten
225 ml / 8 fl. oz / ¾ cup double (heavy) cream
2 tbsp icing (confectioners') sugar
½ tsp vanilla extract
150 g / 5 oz dark chocolate (min. 60% cocoa solids), melted

Hot chocolate orange profiteroles
Add a few drops of natural orange essence to the melted
hot chocolate before drizzling it over the profiteroles.

- Preheat the oven to 200°C (180°C fan) / 400F / gas 6.
- Line a baking tray with greaseproof paper and spray with
  a little water.
- Melt the butter with 150 ml / 5 ⅓ fl. oz / ⅔ cup water and
  bring to the boil.
- Immediately beat in the flour, off the heat, with a wooden
  spoon until it forms a smooth ball of pastry.
- Incorporate the egg a little at a time to make a glossy
  paste.
- Spoon the pastry into a piping bag fitted with a large
  plain nozzle and pipe 2.5 cm (1 in) buns onto the baking
  tray.
- Bake for 20 minutes, increasing the temperature to
  220°C (200°C fan) / 425F / gas 7 halfway through.
- Transfer the profiteroles to a wire rack and make a hole
  in the underneath of each one so the steam can escape.
  Leave to cool completely.
- Whip the cream with the icing sugar and vanilla
  until thick, then spoon it into a piping bag and fill the
  profiteroles through the steam hole. Drizzle the hot
  melted chocolate over the profiteroles and leave to set.

Apricot-glazed apple pie

PREPARATION TIME: **55 minutes**
COOKING TIME: **40–45 minutes**
SERVES: **6–8**

125 g / 4 ⅓ oz / ½ cup caster (superfine) sugar
2 tbsp plain (all-purpose) flour
½ tsp ground cinnamon
800 g / 1 lb 12 oz Bramley apples, peeled, cored and cut into slices

FOR THE PASTRY
200 g / 7 oz / 1 ⅓ cups plain (all-purpose) flour
100 g / 3 ½ oz / ½ cup butter, chilled

APRICOT GLAZE
150 g / 5 oz / ⅔ cup apricot preserves
1 tbsp water

- To make the glaze, heat the apricot preserves in a small saucepan until almost boiling. Remove from the heat and strain so there are no lumps. Incorporate the water and set to one side.

- For the pastry, sieve the flour into a bowl then grate in the butter and mix well.

- Mix in enough cold water to form a dough then wrap it in cling film and chill for 30 minutes.

- Preheat the oven to 190°C (170°C fan) / 375F / gas 5 and butter a 23 cm (9 in) round pie tin.

- Mix the sugar, flour and cinnamon together in a bowl then toss with the apples.

- Roll out the pastry and line the prepared pie tin.

- Arrange the apples on the pastry case and brush over the apricot glaze. Cut away the excess pastry from around the outside.

- Bake the pie for 40–45 minutes. The pastry should be crisp and golden brown and starting to shrink away from the edge of the tin.

Classic apple pie

Lime and coconut popsicles

PREPARATION TIME: **45 minutes**
COOKING TIME: **40–45 minutes**
SERVES: **6–8**

125 g / 4 ⅓ oz / ½ cup caster (superfine) sugar

½ tsp ground cinnamon

800 g / 1 lb12 oz Bramley apples, peeled, cored and cut into thin slices

1 egg, beaten

FOR THE PASTRY
300 g / 10 ½ oz / 2 cups plain (all-purpose) flour

150 g / 5 ½ oz / ⅔ cup butter, chilled

- Sieve the flour into a bowl then grate in the butter and mix well.
- Mix in enough cold water to form a pliable dough then wrap it in cling film and chill for 30 minutes.
- Preheat the oven to 190°C (170°C fan) / 375F / gas 5 and butter a 23 cm round or ridged pie tin.
- Mix the sugar and cinnamon together in a bowl then toss with the apples.
- Roll out half of the pastry and use it to line the prepared pie tin.
- Layer the apples in the pastry case until the apples resemble a rose-like pattern.
- Brush the top layer with beaten egg.
- Bake the pie for 35-45 minutes. The pastry and apples should be golden brown and starting to crisp on top.

PREPARATION TIME: **2 minutes**
FREEZING TIME: **Overnight**
MAKES: **10**

400 ml / 14 fl. oz can coconut milk

7 limes, juiced

2 limes, zested

5 tbsp caster (superfine) sugar

- Combine the coconut milk, lime juice and zest and the sugar in a large mixing bowl. Mix together until well incorporated.
- Divide the mixture between the ice-lolly moulds and insert a stick into the middle of each.
- Leave overnight to freeze.

Lime, mint and coconut popsicles
Add a handful of chopped mint leaves to the mixture before freezing.

THE
COOKERY
COLLECTION

Mini meringue pies

PREPARATION TIME: **1 hour**
COOKING TIME: **45 minutes**
MAKES: **6**

200 g / 7 oz / ¾ cup butter, cubed and chilled
400 g / 14 oz / 1 ⅔ cups plain (all-purpose) flour

FOR THE MERINGUE
4 large eggs, separated, whites
110 g / 4 oz / ½ cup caster (superfine) sugar
1 tsp cornflour (cornstarch)

> **Mini jam meringue pies**
> Add 1 teaspoon of jam (jelly) to each mini pie before
> piping the meringue into the individual cases.

- Start with the pastry, rub the butter into the flour then stir in just enough cold water to make a dough. Wrap the dough in cling film and chill for 30 minutes.
- Preheat the oven to 200°C (180°C fan) / 400F / gas 6.
- Roll out the pastry on a floured surface and cut out 6 circles to line 6 tartlet tins.
- For the meringue, whisk the egg whites until stiff, then gradually whisk in half the sugar until the mixture is very shiny.
- Fold in the remaining sugar and cornflour then spoon the mixture into a piping bag.
- Pipe the meringue into 6 spirals on each mini pie.
- Bake the meringue pies for 45 minutes or until they are crisp on the outside but still chewy in the middle.
- Transfer the meringue pies to a wire rack to cool.

Custard and vanilla tarts

PREPARATION TIME: **10 minutes**
COOKING TIME: **25–30 minutes**
MAKES: **6**

800 g / 1 lb / 12 oz all-butter puff pastry
3 lemons, juiced
175 g / 6 oz / ¾ cup caster (superfine) sugar
2 tsp cornflour (cornstarch)
4 large eggs, beaten
225 ml / 8 fl. oz / ¾ cup double (heavy) cream
½ tsp vanilla powder
whole vanilla pods, to garnish

- Preheat the oven to 200°C (180°C fan) / 400F / gas 6.
- Roll out the pastry on a lightly floured surface and cut out 6 large circles with a pastry cutter then bake for 10 minutes.
- Remove the pastry cases from the oven and reduce the heat to 160°C (140°C fan) / 325F / gas 3.
- Stir the lemon juice into the caster sugar and cornflour to dissolve, then whisk in the eggs, cream and vanilla powder.
- Strain the mixture into the pastry cases and bake for 15–20 minutes or until just set in the middle.
- Use a blowtorch to give the tarts a slightly burnt finish.
- Serve with some vanilla pods on the side.

Apple and raisin turnovers

PREPARATION TIME: **30 minutes**
COOKING TIME: **18 minutes**
MAKES: **6**

3 large cooking apples, peeled and diced
75 g / 2 ⅔ oz / ⅓ cup raisins
3 tbsp caster (superfine) sugar
800 g / 1 lb 12 oz all-butter puff pastry
1 egg, beaten

- Preheat the oven to 220°C (200°C fan) / 425F / gas 7.
- Put the apples, raisins and sugar in a saucepan with 4 tablespoons of cold water.
- Put a lid on the pan then cook over a gentle heat for 10 minutes, stirring occasionally. Leave to cool.
- Roll out the pastry on a lightly floured surface and cut out 6 large circles with a fluted pastry cutter.
- Add a tablespoon of apple and raisin compote to the middle of each one and brush round the edge with egg.
- Fold the pastry in half and press the edges to seal, then score a pattern into the top.
- Brush the turnovers with egg and bake for 18 minutes or until golden brown and cooked through.
- Once cooked, leave to cool then serve.

Apple and cranberry turnovers
Replace the raisins with the same amount of dried cranberries for a heavenly variation.

Passion fruit cheesecake

PREPARATION TIME: **20 minutes**
COOKING TIME: **40–50 minutes**
CHILLING TIME: **3 hours**
SERVES: **12**

200 g / 7 oz digestive biscuits, crushed
2 tbsp desiccated coconut
3 tbsp butter, melted

FOR THE FILLING
600 g / 1 lb 5 oz / 2 ½ cups cream cheese
150 ml / 5 ⅓ fl. oz / ⅔ cup coconut milk
175 g / 6 oz / ¾ cup caster (superfine) sugar
2 large eggs, plus 1 egg yolk
2 tbsp plain (all-purpose) flour
4 tbsp desiccated coconut

FOR THE TOPPING
1 large mango, peeled and sliced
4 passion fruit, pulp sieved to remove the seeds

- Preheat the oven to 180°C (160°C fan) / 350F / gas 4 and grease a 20 cm (8 in) round spring-form cake tin.
- Mix the biscuit crumbs with the coconut and butter and press into an even layer in the bottom of the tin.
- Bake the biscuit layer for 5 minutes or until firm.
- Whisk together the filling ingredients until smooth. Spoon the cheesecake mixture on top of the biscuit base, levelling the top with a palette knife.
- Bake the cheesecake for 40–50 minutes or until the middle is only just set.
- Leave to cool in the tin then chill in the refrigerator for 3 hours.
- When you are ready to serve, blend the mango to a smooth pulp and mix in the passion fruit seeds. Spoon over the cheesecake and level the topping using a spoon.

Raspberry cheesecake
Replace the passion fruit with crushed frozen raspberries to add a delicious, sweet layer.

Apple and blackberry strudel bites

PREPARATION TIME: 20 minutes
COOKING TIME: 18–20 minutes
MAKES: 12–18

3 large cooking apples, peeled and diced
50 g / 1 ¾ oz / ⅓ cup blackberries, washed
3 tbsp caster (superfine) sugar
1 tsp mixed spice
800 g / 1 lb 12 oz all-butter puff pastry
1 egg, beaten
2 tbsp light brown sugar
icing (confectioners') sugar, to serve

- Preheat the oven to 220°C (200°C fan) / 425F / gas 7.
- Put the apples, blackberries, sugar and spice in a saucepan with 4 tablespoons of cold water.
- Put a lid on the pan then cook over a gentle heat for 10 minutes, stirring occasionally. Leave to cool.
- Roll out the pastry on a lightly floured surface and cut into 6 squares.
- Add a heaped tablespoon of apple and blackberry compote to the middle of each one. Roll the pastry until the mixture is completely concealed. Brush with the egg and sprinkle with brown sugar.
- Transfer to a baking tray and bake for 18 minutes or until golden brown and cooked through.
- Remove from the oven and cut into mini bite-sized slices. Sprinkle with icing sugar to serve.

Apple and raisin strudel bites
Follow the same method but replace the blackcurrants for 75 g / 2 ⅔ oz / ⅓ cup raisins.

Summer berry meringue nests

PREPARATION TIME: **15 minutes**
COOKING TIME: **45 minutes**
CHILLING TIME: **1 hour**
MAKES: **18**

225 ml / 8 fl. oz / ¾ cup double (heavy) cream
½ tsp vanilla extract
100 g / 3 ½ oz strawberries, quartered
100 g / 3 ½ oz / ⅔ cup blueberries
mint leaves, to garnish

FOR THE MERINGUE
4 large eggs, separated, whites
110 g / 4 oz / ½ cup caster (superfine) sugar
1 tsp cornflour (cornstarch)

- Preheat the oven to 140°C (120°C fan) / 275F / gas 1 and oil and line a baking tray with greaseproof paper.
- To make the meringues, whisk the egg whites until stiff, then gradually whisk in half the sugar until the mixture is very shiny.
- Fold in the remaining sugar and cornflour then spoon the mixture into a piping bag. Pipe the meringue into 6 nests on the prepared baking tray.
- Bake the meringues for 45 minutes or until they are crisp on the outside, but still a bit chewy in the middle, then leave to cool completely.
- While the meringues are cooking, heat the cream and vanilla extract to simmering point, then stir until smooth. Chill for 1 hour.
- Whip the vanilla cream until thick then spoon it into a piping bag, fitted with a plain nozzle.
- Pipe a spiral of cream on top of each meringue nest and decorate with the berries and mint leaves.

White chocolate berry meringue nests
Grate a bar of white chocolate and sprinkle the shavings on top of each meringue.

Chia berry pudding

PREPARATION TIME: **35 Minutes**
SERVES: **4**

4 tbsp chia seeds
2 tbsp maple syrup
1 tsp vanilla powder
1.2 litres / 2 pints / 4 ½ cups dairy-free almond or rice milk
a handful of fresh raspberries and blueberries, to garnish
fresh mint leaves, to garnish

- Combine the chia seeds, maple syrup, vanilla powder and milk in a large bowl. Mix thoroughly and leave in the fridge for 30 minutes to set.
- Once the chia seeds have expanded and the mixture has doubled in size, divide between four serving glasses.
- Garnish with some fresh berries and mint leaves. Serve cold.

Chia berry chocolate pudding
Add 2 tbsp cacao powder and a pinch of salt to the mixture for a yummy chocolate version.

Forest fruit crumble pots

PREPARATION TIME: 10 minutes
COOKING TIME: 25 minutes
SERVES: 6

200 g / 7 oz / 1 ⅓ cups blackberries
200 g / 7 oz / 1 ⅓ cups raspberries
4 tbsp caster (superfine) sugar
75 g / 2 ⅔ oz / ⅓ cup butter
50 g / 1 ¾ oz / ⅓ cup plain (all-purpose) flour
1 tbsp ground almonds
1 ½ tbsp light brown sugar
fresh mint leaves, to garnish

- Preheat the oven to 180°C (160°C fan) / 350F / gas 4.
- Mix the blackberries and raspberries with the sugar and divide them between 6 ramekin dishes.
- Rub the butter into the flour and stir in the ground almonds and brown sugar.
- Crumble the mixture over the fruit then bake for 25 minutes or until the topping is golden brown.
- Garnish with the fresh mint leaves.
- Delicious served with ice cream and raspberry sauce.

Vegan fruit crumble pots
Replace the butter with the same amount of dairy-free butter for a tasty vegan alternative. Serve with some vegan ice cream on the side.

Superfood lollies

PREPARATION TIME: **5 minutes**
FREEZING TIME: **Overnight**
MAKES: **10 lollies**

400 ml / 14 fl. oz can coconut milk

7 limes, juiced

2 limes, zested

4 tbsp agave nectar

4 tbsp chia seeds

1 tbsp maca powder

- Combine all the ingredients in a large mixing bowl. Mix together until well incorporated.
- Divide the mixture between the ice-lolly moulds and insert a stick into the middle of each.
- Leave overnight to freeze.

Super berry popsicles
Add a handful of crushed frozen raspberries to the mixture before freezing. Swap out the maca powder for the same amount of acai berry powder.

Chia and apricot dessert

PREPARATION TIME: **35 Minutes**
SERVES: **4**

4 tbsp chia seeds

2 tbsp maple syrup

1 tsp vanilla powder

1.2 litres / 2 pints / 4 ½ cups dairy-free almond or rice milk

2 apricots, stones removed and sliced

redcurrants, to garnish

fresh mint leaves, to garnish

- Combine the chia seeds, maple syrup, vanilla powder and milk in a large bowl. Mix thoroughly and leave in the fridge for 30 minutes to set.
- Once the chia seeds have expanded and the mixture has doubled in size, divide between four serving glasses.
- Garnish with the apricot slices and redcurrants. Serve cold.

Chia peach pudding
Replace the sliced apricot with sliced peach for a slightly sweeter variation.

Index

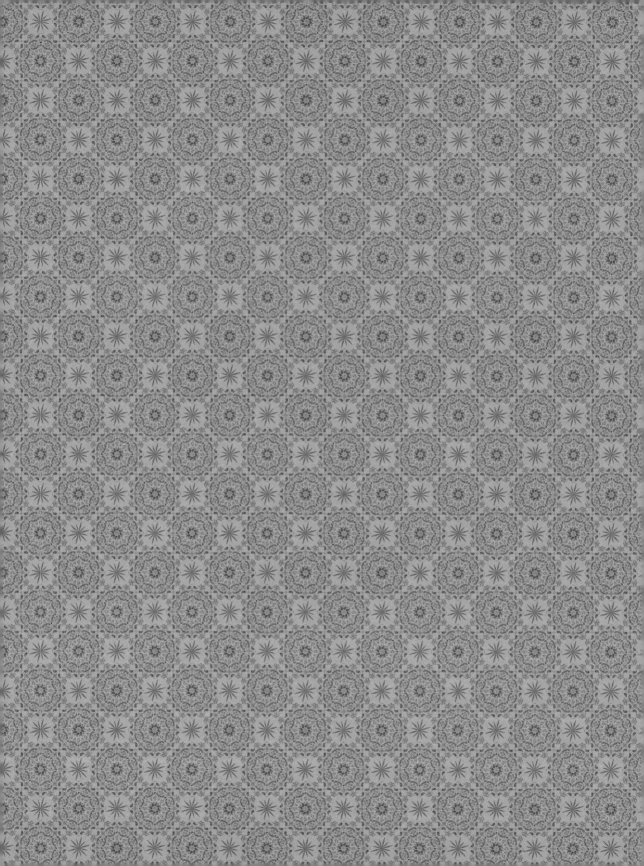